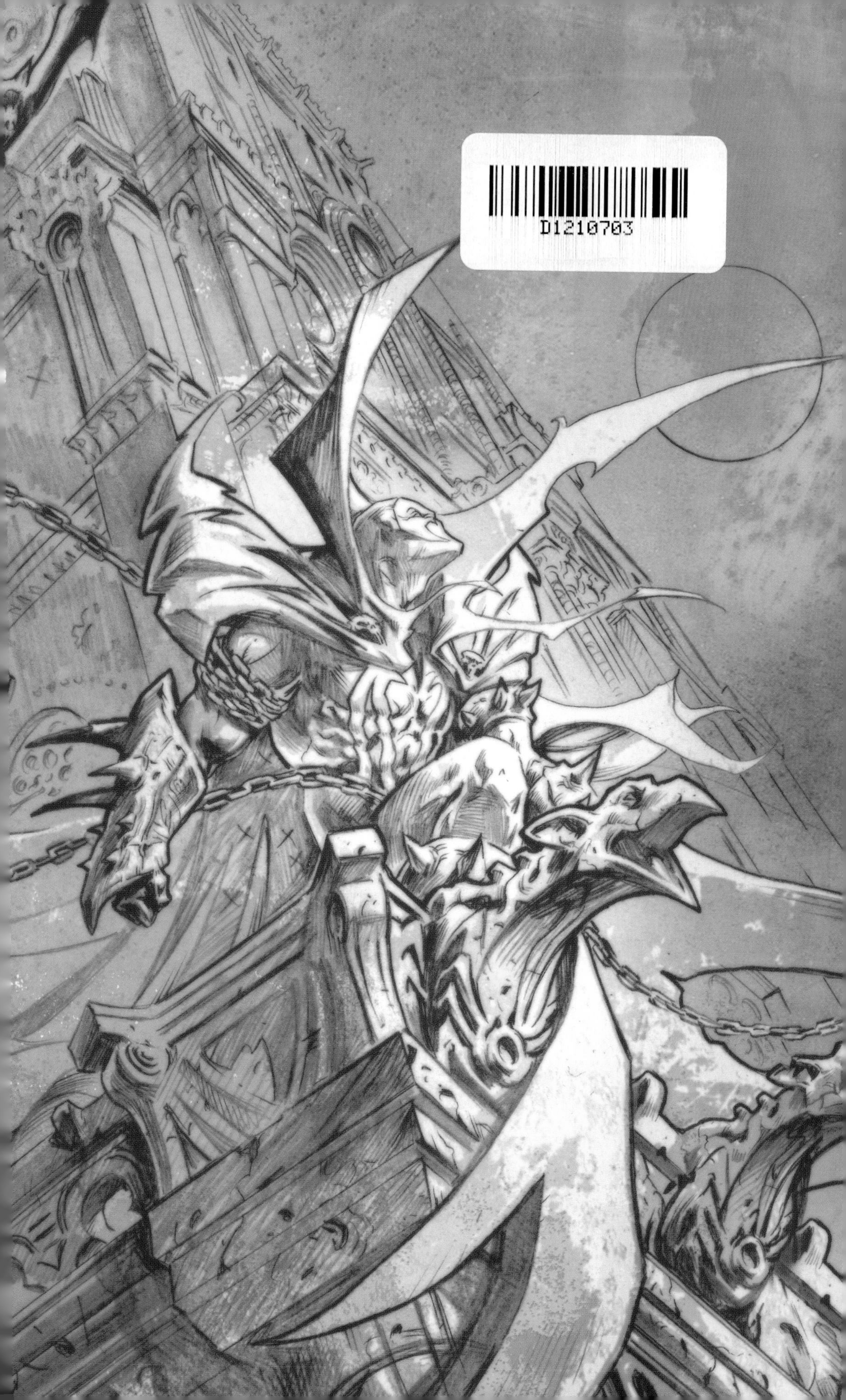

SIMONY HISTORY

Semic, the publisher of French versions of *Spawn* and many other American comics, published an original Spawn story, *Spawn: Simony* — written and illustrated by a French creative team made up of Jean-François Porcherot, Alex Nikolavitch and Aleksi Briclot – in 2003. The book you're now holding is the English translation of the comic now available in the United States for the first time.

The story came as a result of Semic seeking to continue the special events it has organized around Spawn since 1999. "For nearly 10 years, Todd McFarlane Productions and Semic have enjoyed an exceptionally good relationship, which has led to various joint projects, such as a cover drawn by renowned French artist J.Y. Mitton for *Spawn* #46 [French edition] in 2000," Porcherot said. "A year later, Semic published *Spawn* #57, which included the U.S. edition of *Spawn* #100. To celebrate this special event, Semic organized an exhibit of its original art at Album, the largest comic book store in France. Concurrently, Semic arranged for French cable TV channel Canal Jimmy to program a 'Spawn Night' featuring all three seasons of the HBO animated series. The same year, *Spawn* artist Angel Medina was Semic's guest for the Angoulême International Comics Festival. In 2003, Todd McFarlane was Angoulême's Guest of Honor during its 30th festival.

It was there that the "French Spawn Project" was officially launched.

The project originally came to life when Semic Editor-in-Chief Thierry Mornet met with Spawn creator Todd McFarlane at the San Diego Comic-Con International in 2002. At the meeting, Mornet pitched the idea to McFarlane, based on the plot by Porcherot and art samples by Briclot.

"Todd gave his agreement and all the details were worked out when he came to Angoulême in January," Porcherot said. The story, titled "Simony," is 44 pages long, and fully drawn, inked and painted by Briclot, while Alex developed the story based on Porcherot's plot. It was initially published in June and August of 2003 in France in the *Spawn* bimonthly comic there.

The story involves former Hellspawn and current Spawn mentor Cogliostro in a scheme to rid himself of his Hellspawn curse. The events depicted in the story take place after issue #100 and before Al Simmons became "separated" from his Spawn counterpart.

Cog — with the help of a young woman — gathers ancient religious artifacts which played a major role in human history 2000 years ago. The action shifts from the Far East to Paris, where the French government's security service is also looking for one of the artifacts to breed its own super-soldier and eventually sell the technology. That secret project is located in the Paris catacombs and combines science and sorcery. Some religious orders seek to destroy this project because it could cast a new light on the true identity of one of Christianity's most sacred icons. Cog must have the artifact to obtain redemption and Spawn wants to stop the madness of it all. These characters and their conflicting agendas eventually collide in Paris under the eye of Mammon, the man-in-white in charge of Hell.

This is one of the few times Todd McFarlane has allowed an outside publishing company to create and publish an original *Spawn* story.

"My company and Semic have had a great long-term business relationship," said McFarlane. "When they came to me with this story and I took a look at the artwork, it was a done deal. I was really impressed with the textures and depth of the art and the story; very unique, but still very appropriate to our idea of what the Spawn universe should be."

TODD McFARLANE AND
IMAGE COMICS PRESENT

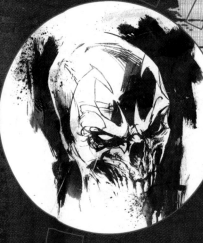

SPAWN
Simony

SEMIC STUDIOS

SYNOPSIS
JEAN-FRANÇOIS PORCHEROT

WRITER
ALEX NIKOLAVITCH

ARTIST
ALEKSI BRICLOT

LETTERING (French version)
HERVÉ GRAIZON from SEMIC STUDIOS

EDITORS
JEAN-FRANÇOIS PORCHEROT & THIERRY MORNET

EDITOR-IN-CHIEF
THIERRY MORNET

TODD McFARLANE PRODUCTIONS

PRESIDENT OF
ENTERTAINMENT
TERRY FITZGERALD

MANAGER OF
INTERNATIONAL PUBLISHING
SUZY THOMAS

PRODUCTION MANAGER
TYLER JEFFERS

LETTERING
JIMMY BETANCOURT

ART DIRECTOR
JASON GONZALEZ

PUBLISHER FOR
IMAGE COMICS
ERIK LARSEN

SPECIAL THANKS TO
AND TRANSLATION BY
BOB McFARLANE

SPAWN CREATED BY
TODD McFARLANE

TODD McFARLANE PRODUCTIONS
SPAWN.COM

SPAWN Simony. May 2004. First Printing. Published by IMAGE COMICS 1071 N. Batavia St., Suite A, Orange, CA 92867, $7.95 USA $10.60 CAN.

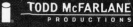

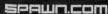

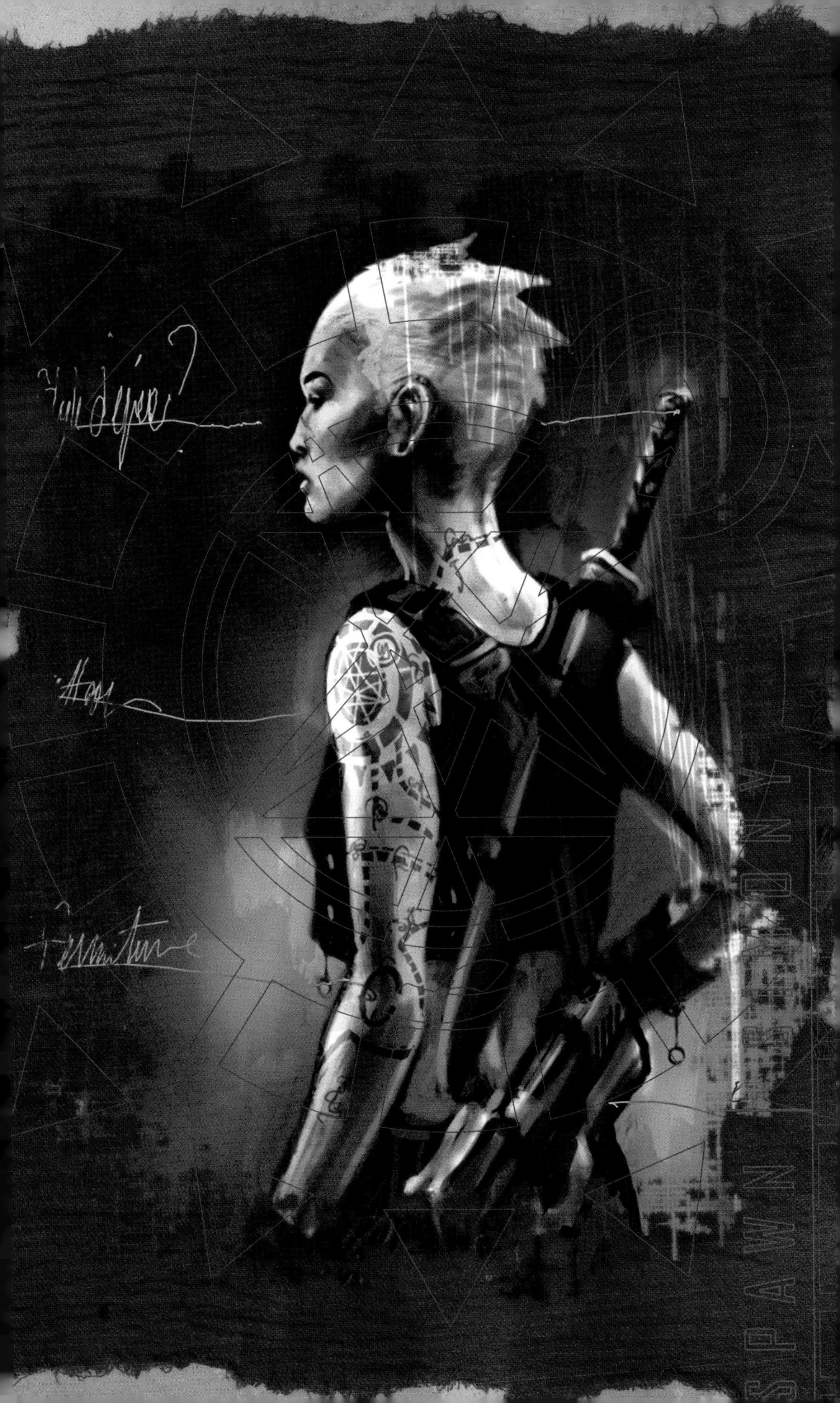

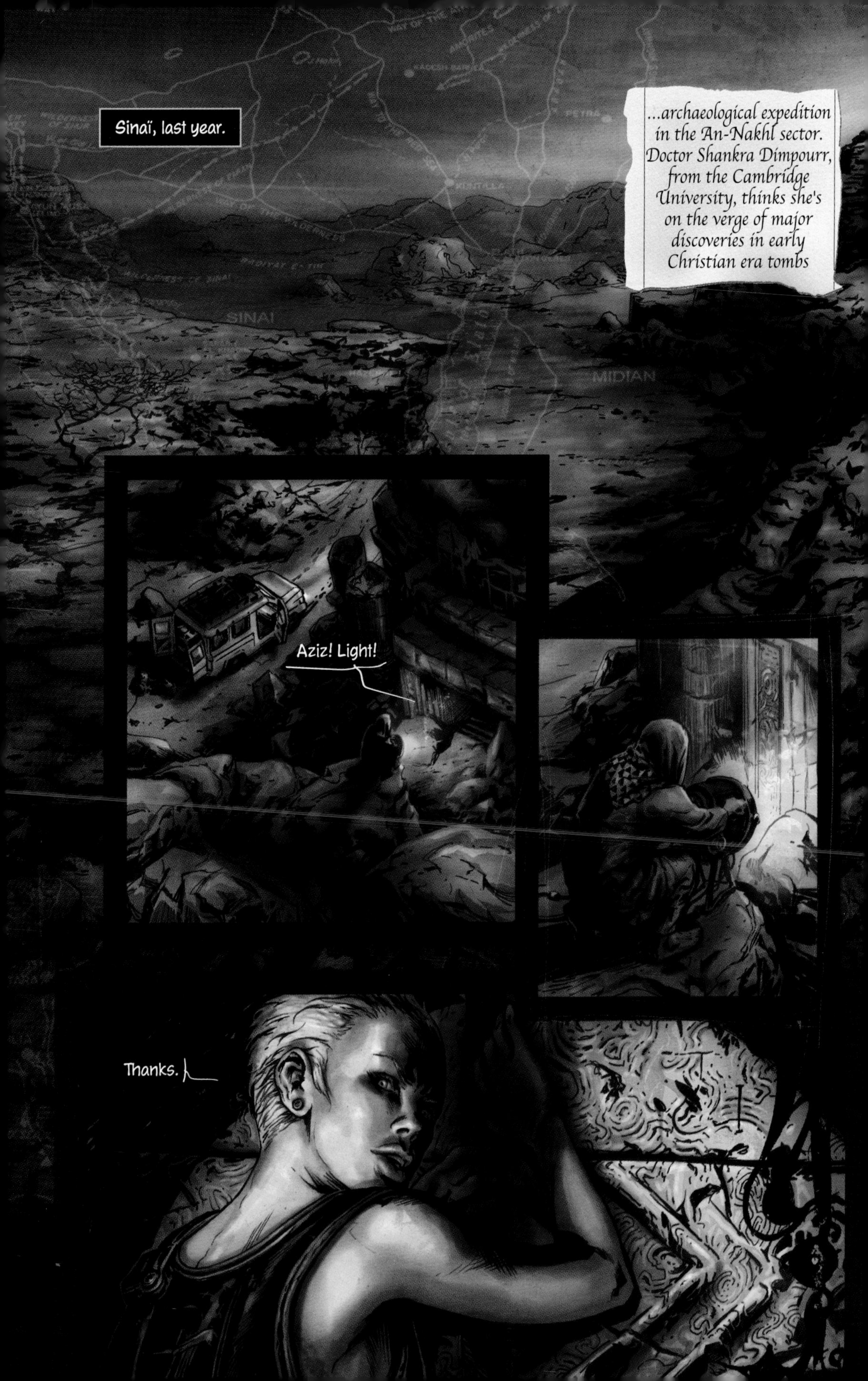
Sinaï, last year.
...archaeological expedition in the An-Nakhl sector. Doctor Shankra Dimpourr, from the Cambridge University, thinks she's on the verge of major discoveries in early Christian era tombs
SINAI
MIDIAN
Aziz! Light!
Thanks.

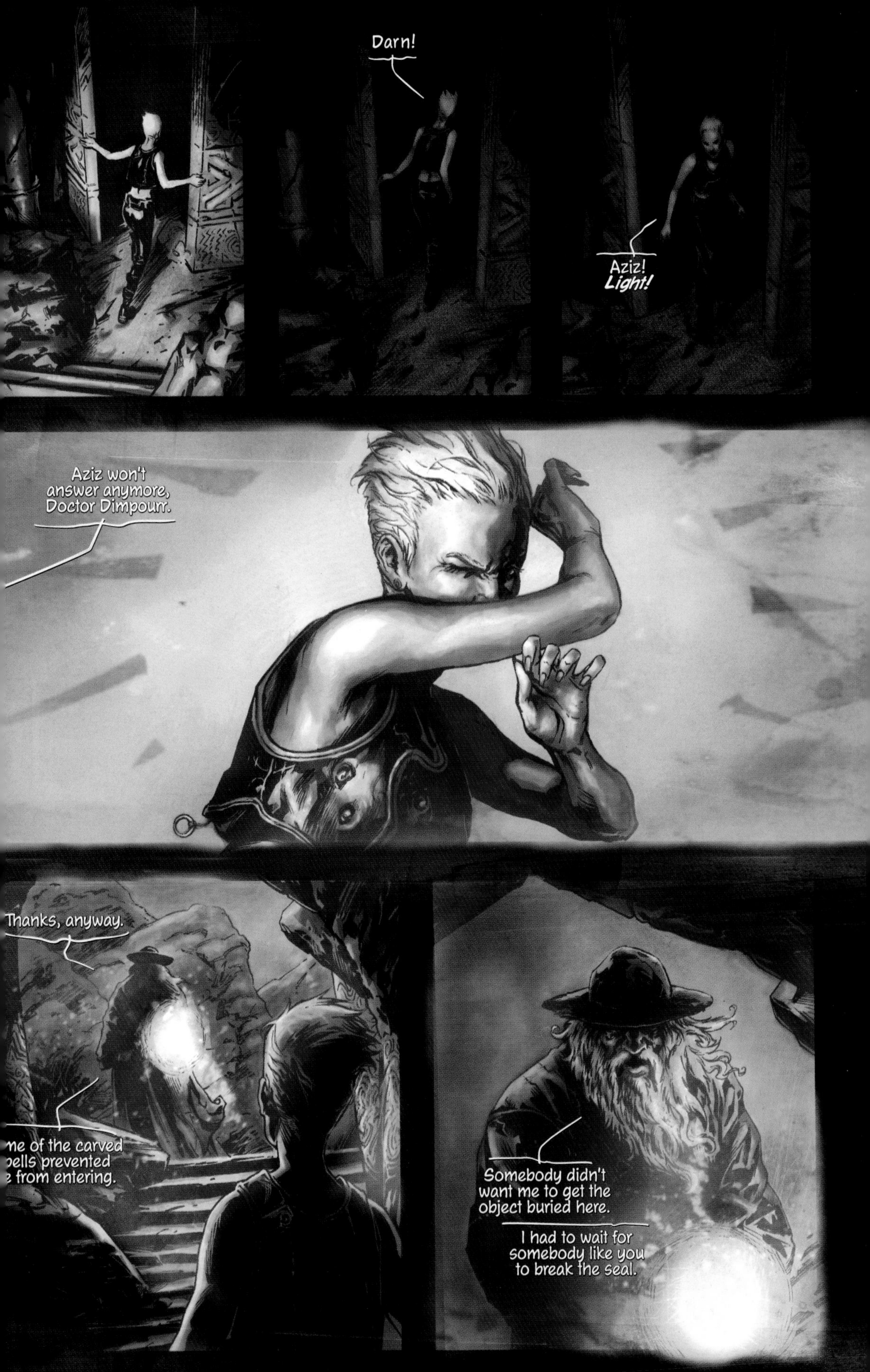
Darn!
Aziz! *Light!*
Aziz won't answer anymore, Doctor Dimpourr.
Thanks, anyway.
me of the carved
pells prevented
e from entering.
Somebody didn't want me to get the object buried here.
I had to wait for somebody like you to break the seal.

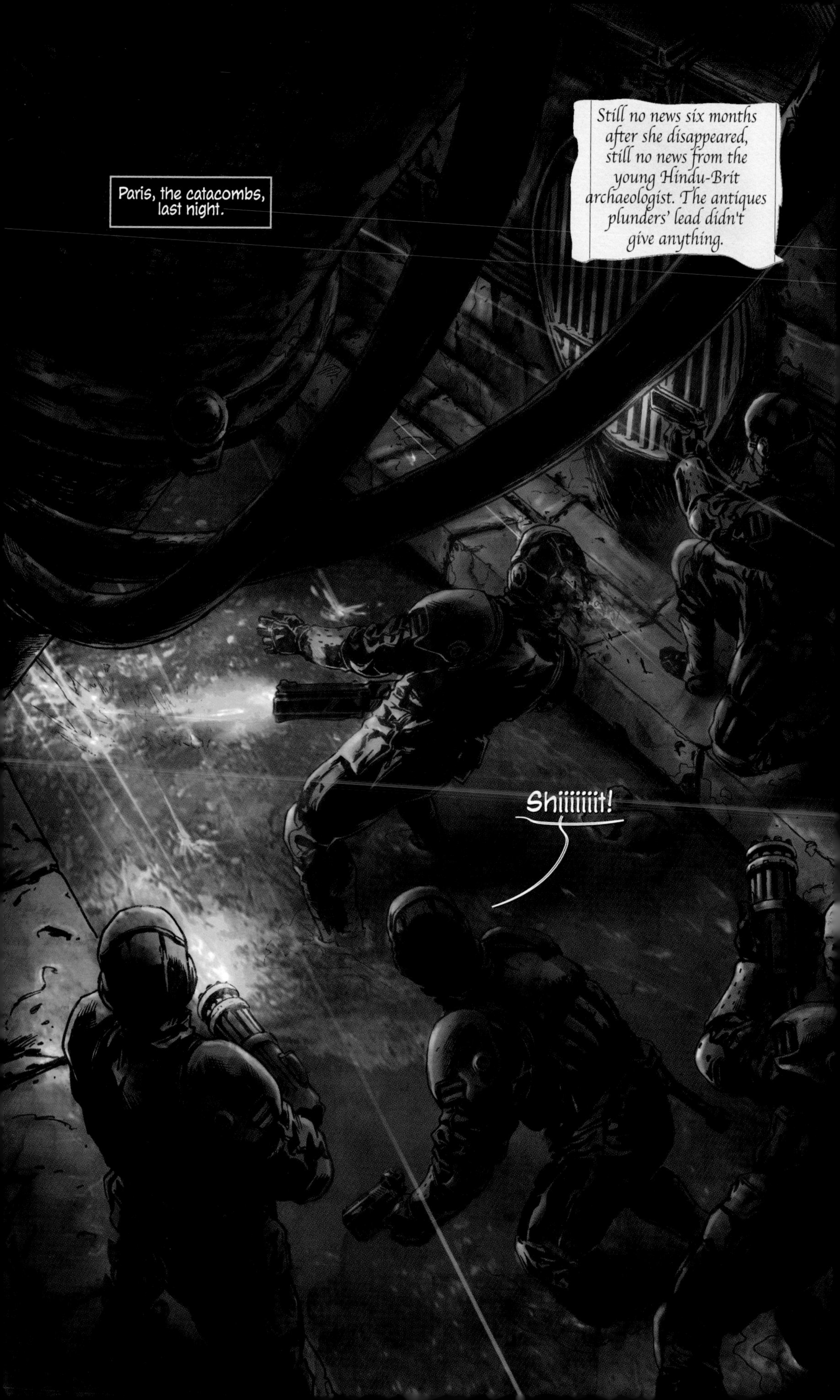
Paris, the catacombs, last night.
Still no news six months after she disappeared, still no news from the young Hindu-Brit archaeologist. The antiques plunders' lead didn't give anything.
Shiiiiiiit!

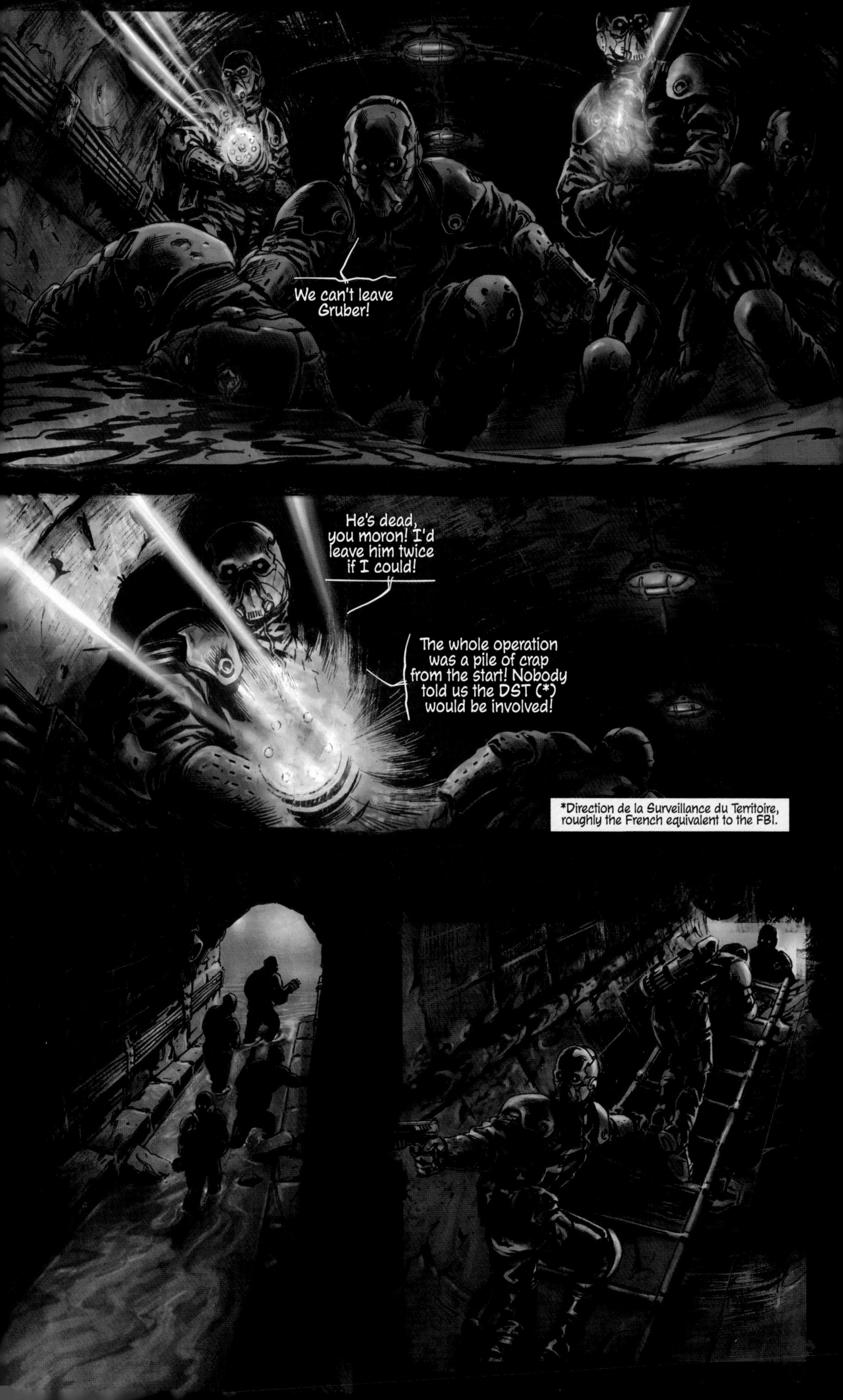
We can't leave Gruber!
He's dead, you moron! I'd leave him twice if I could!
The whole operation was a pile of crap from the start! Nobody told us the DST (*) would be involved!
*Direction de la Surveillance du Territoire, roughly the French equivalent to the FBI.

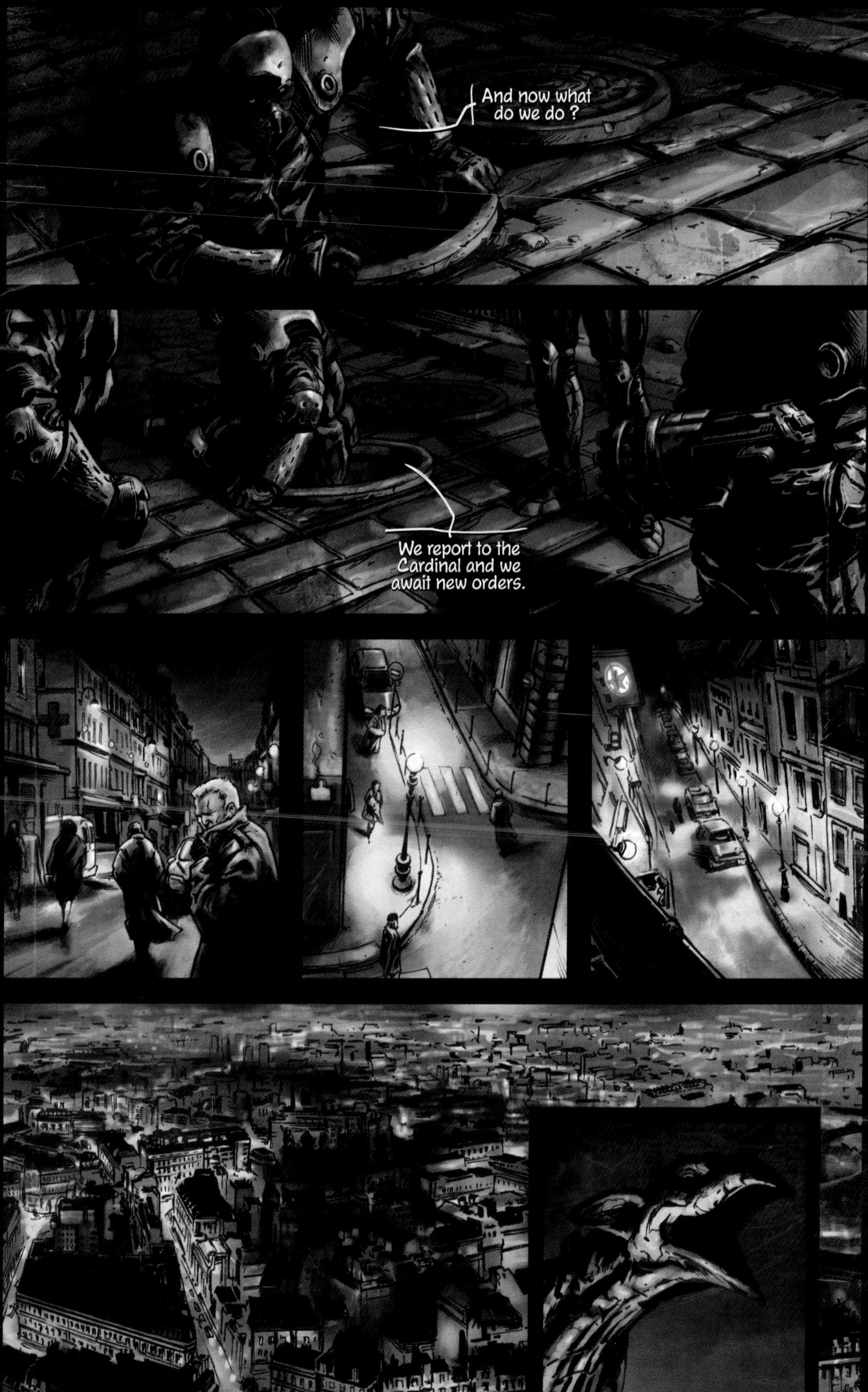
And now what do we do ?
We report to the Cardinal and we await new orders.

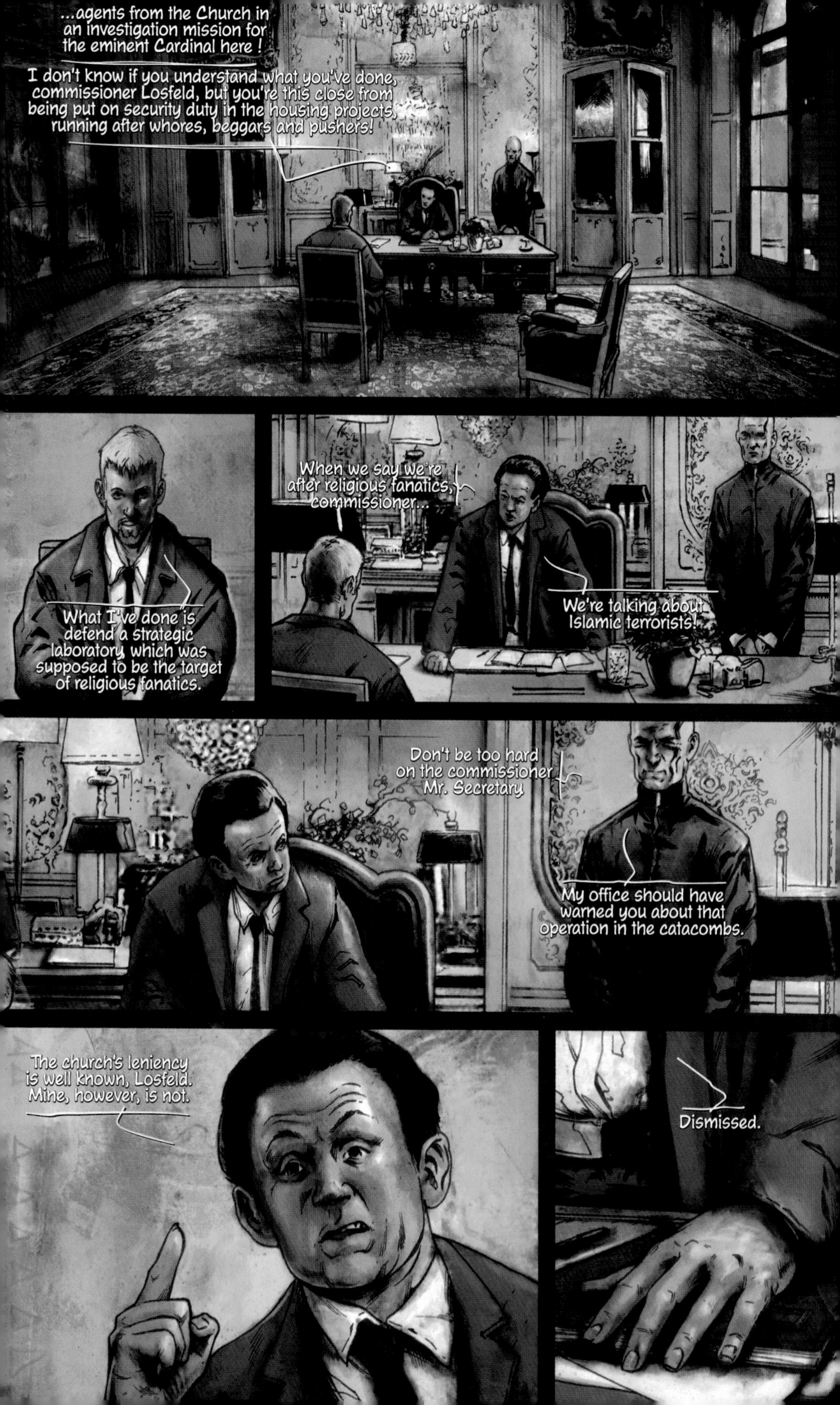
...agents from the Church in an investigation mission for the eminent Cardinal here !
I don't know if you understand what you've done, commissioner Losfeld, but you're this close from being put on security duty in the housing projects, running after whores, beggars and pushers!
What I've done is defend a strategic laboratory which was supposed to be the target of religious fanatics.
When we say we're after religious fanatics, commissioner...
We're talking about Islamic terrorists!
Don't be too hard on the commissioner Mr. Secretary
My office should have warned you about that operation in the catacombs.
The church's leniency is well known, Losfeld. Mine, however, is not.
Dismissed.

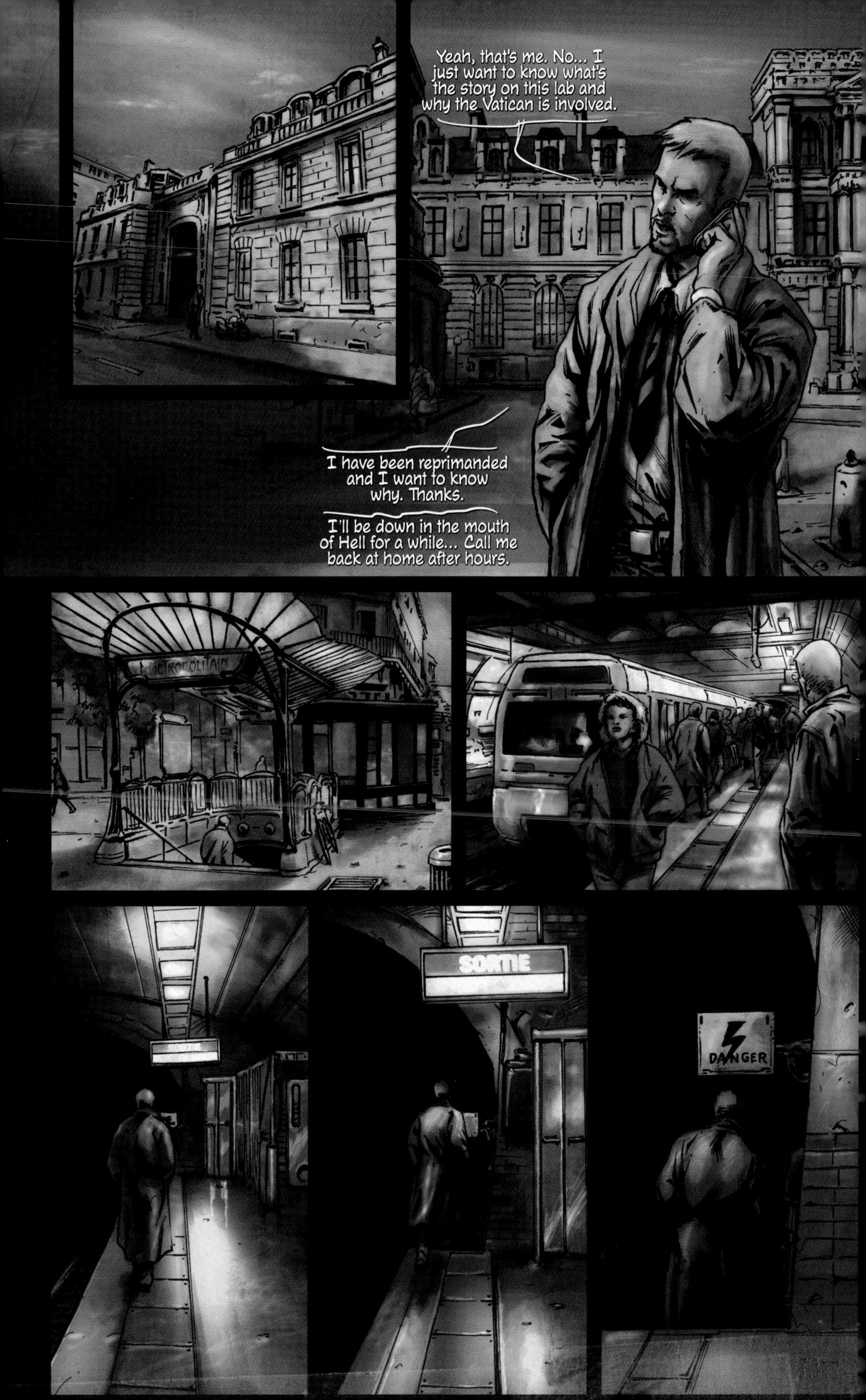
Yeah, that's me. No... I just want to know what's the story on this lab and why the Vatican is involved.
I have been reprimanded and I want to know why. Thanks.
I'll be down in the mouth of Hell for a while... Call me back at home after hours.
SORTIE
DANGER

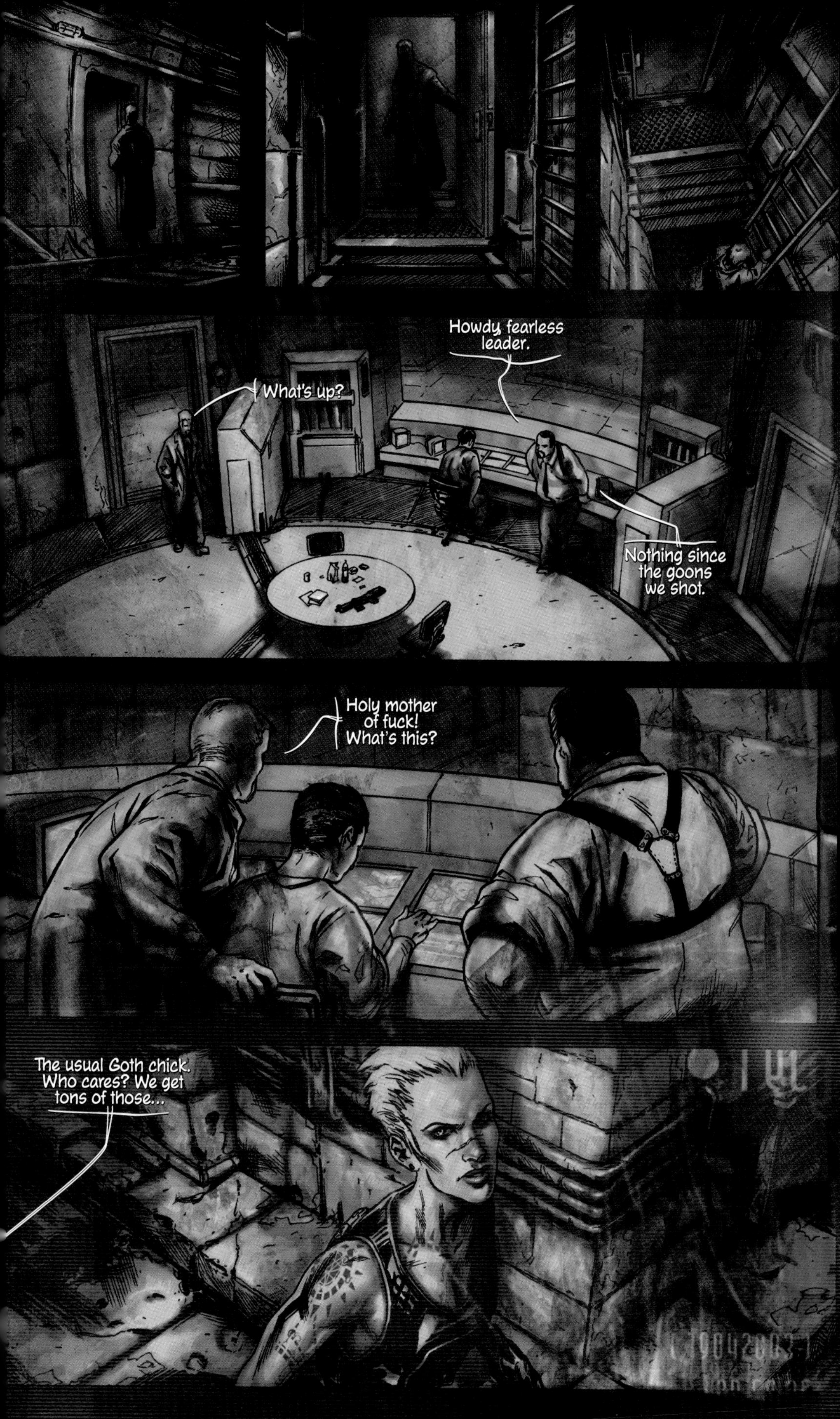
Howdy, fearless leader.
What's up?
Nothing since the goons we shot.
Holy mother of fuck! What's this?
The usual Goth chick. Who cares? We get tons of those...

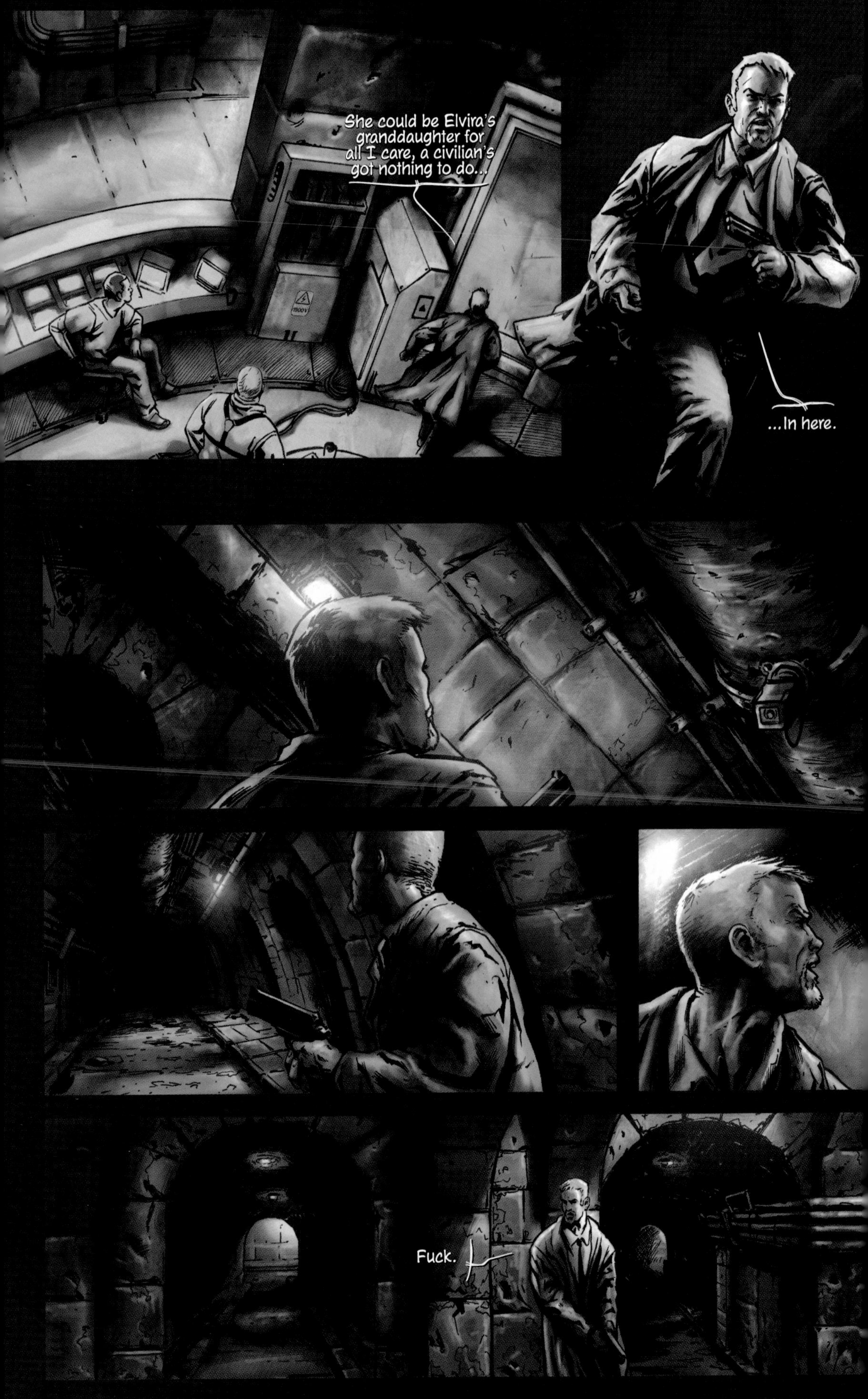
She could be Elvira's granddaughter for all I care, a civilian's got nothing to do...
...In here.
Fuck.

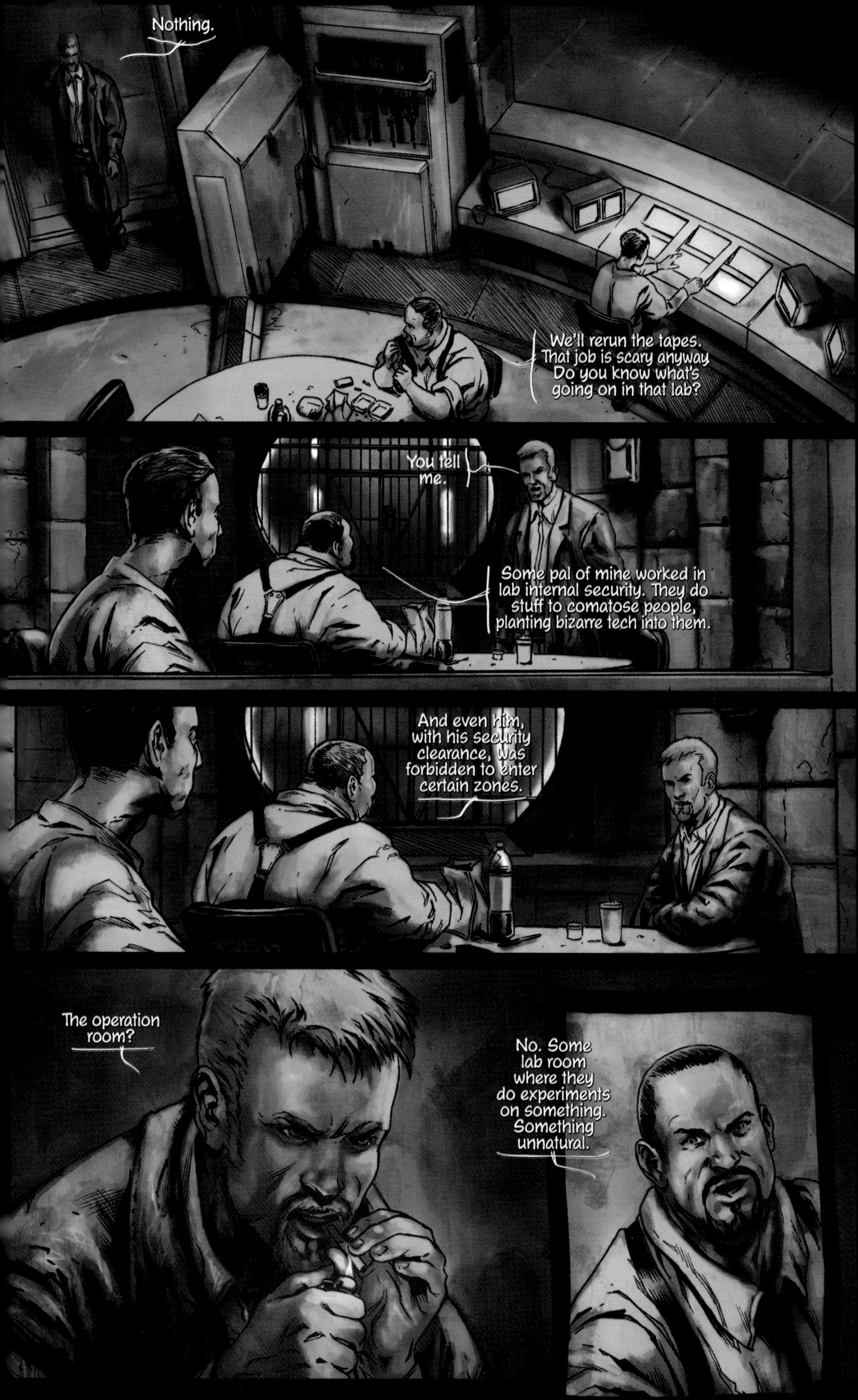

Nothing.
We'll rerun the tapes. That job is scary anyway. Do you know what's going on in that lab?
You tell me.
Some pal of mine worked in lab internal security. They do stuff to comatose people, planting bizarre tech into them.
And even him, with his security clearance, was forbidden to enter certain zones.
The operation room?
No. Some lab room where they do experiments on something. Something unnatural.

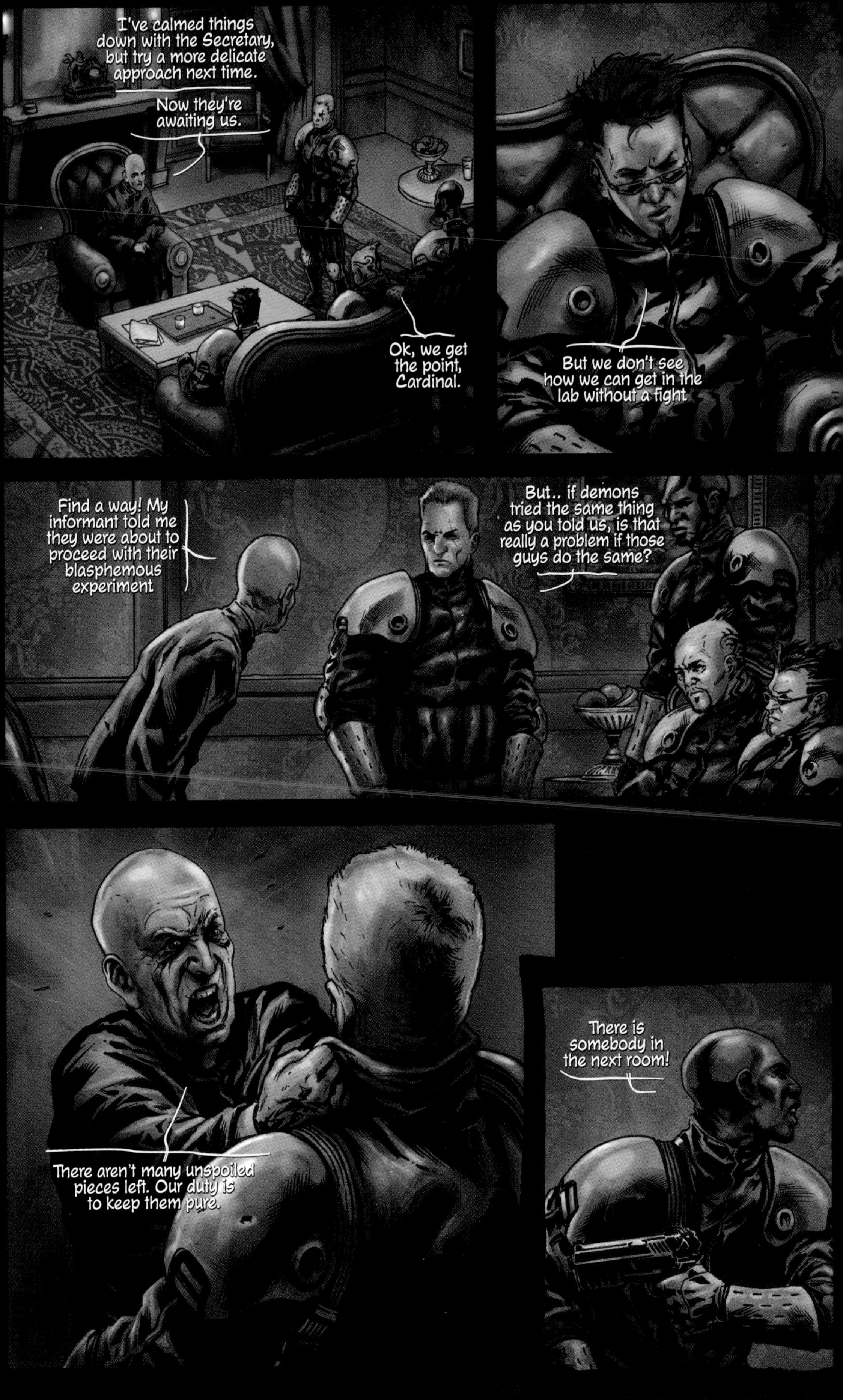
I've calmed things down with the Secretary, but try a more delicate approach next time.
Now they're awaiting us.
Ok, we get the point, Cardinal.
But we don't see how we can get in the lab without a fight
Find a way! My informant told me they were about to proceed with their blasphemous experiment
But.. if demons tried the same thing as you told us, is that really a problem if those guys do the same?
There aren't many unspoiled pieces left. Our duty is to keep them pure.
There is somebody in the next room!

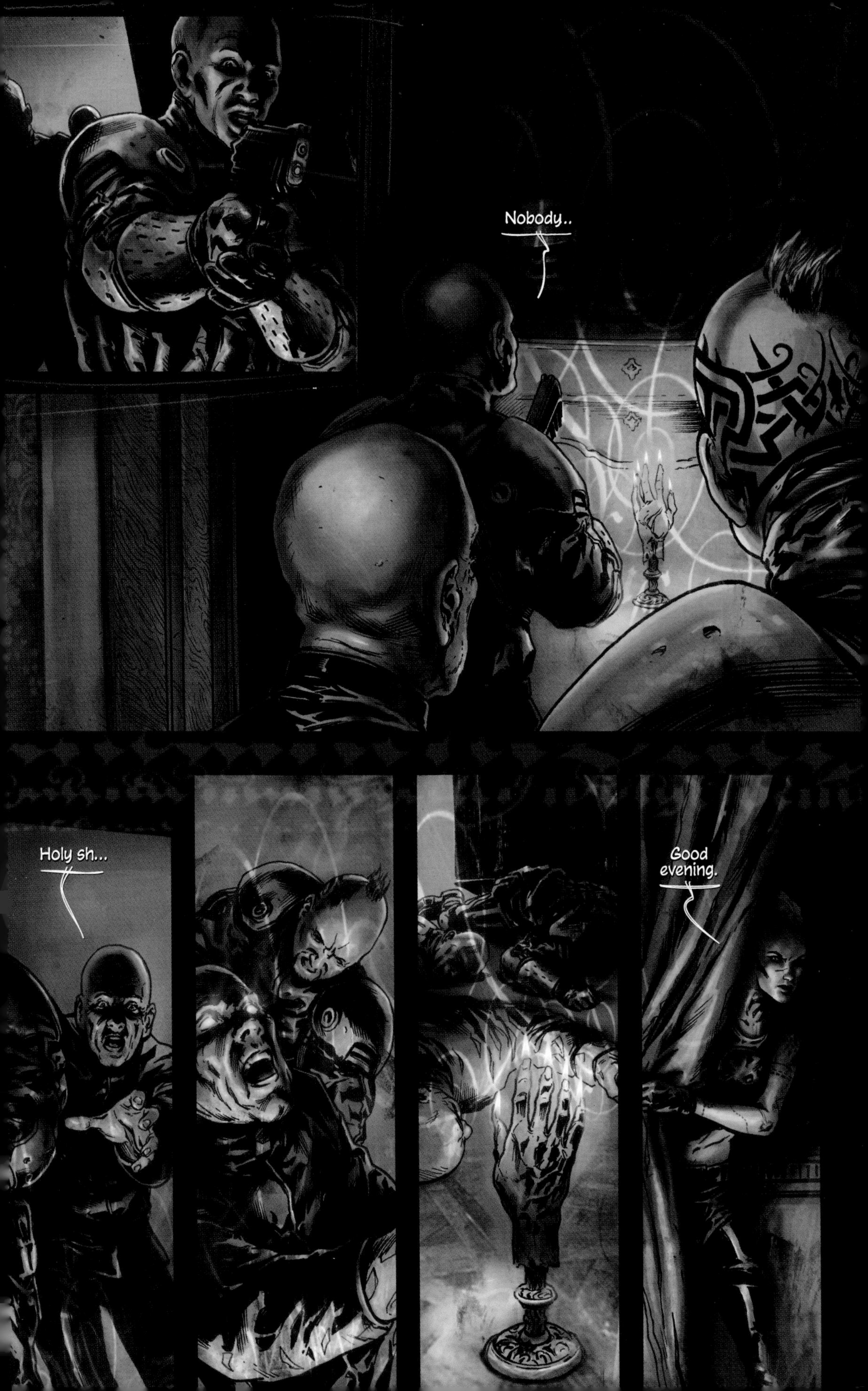
Nobody..
Holy sh...
Good evening.

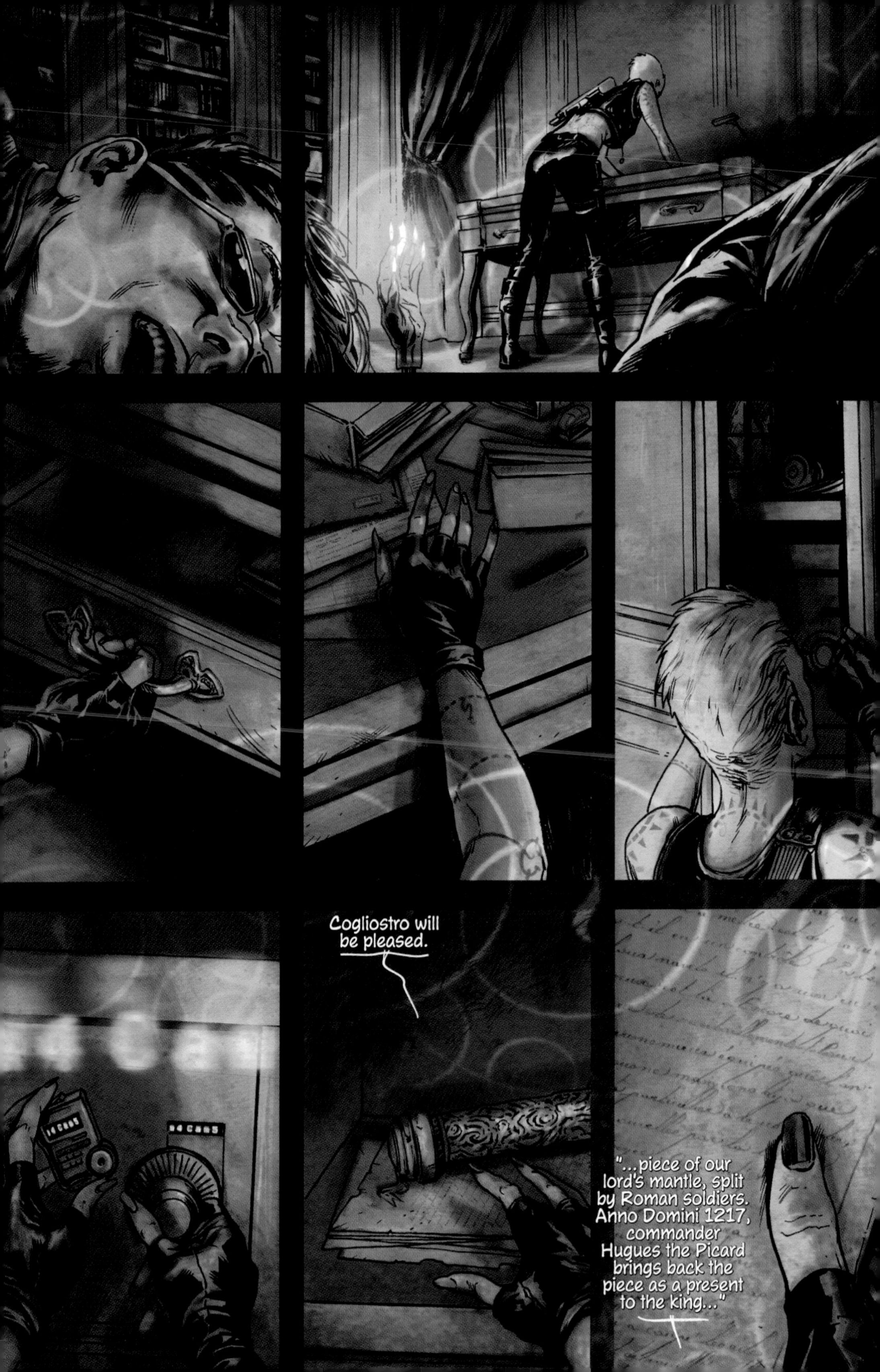
Cogliostro will be pleased.
"...piece of our lord's mantle, split by Roman soldiers. Anno Domini 1217, commander Hugues the Picard brings back the piece as a present to the king..."

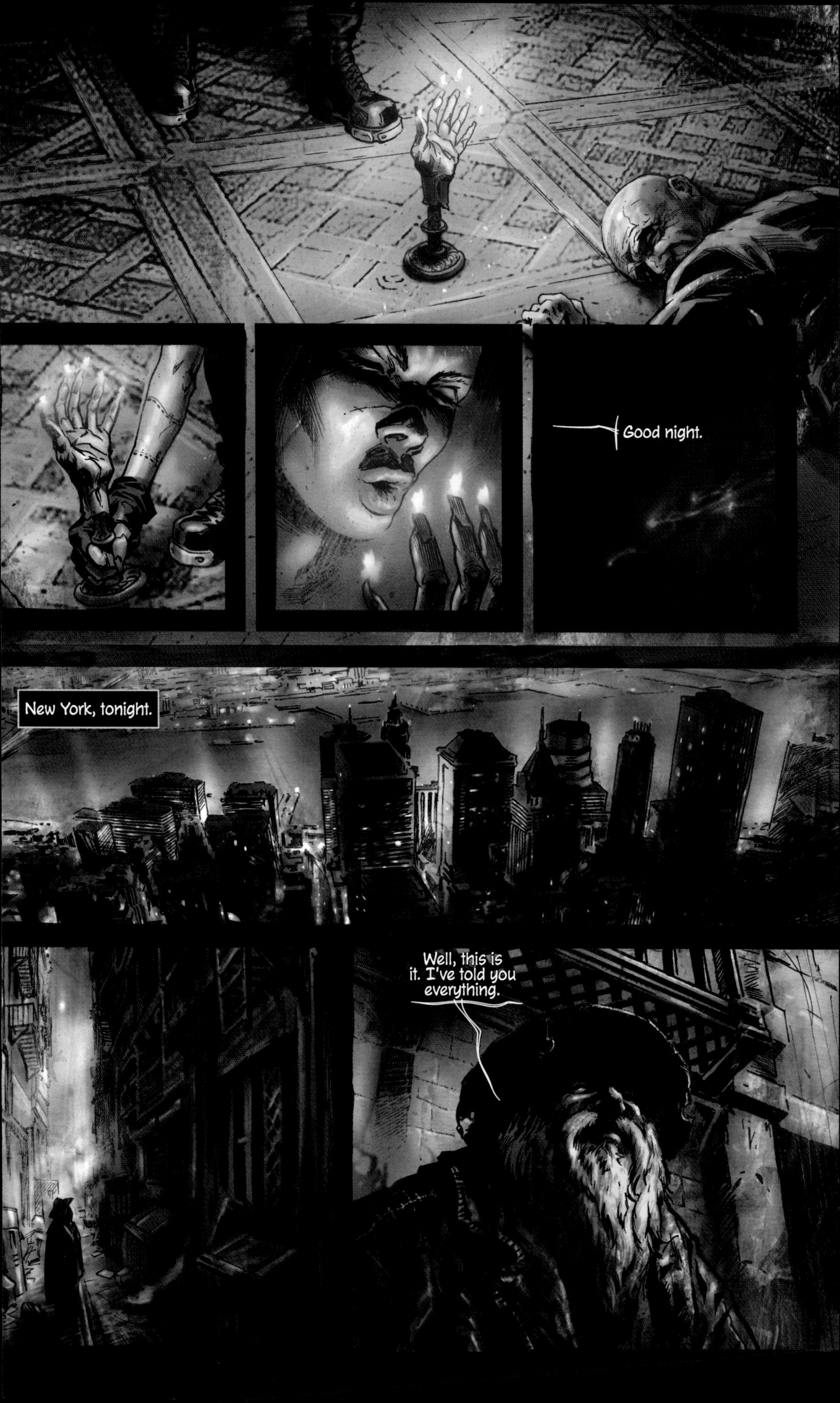

Good night.
New York, tonight.
Well, this is it. I've told you everything.

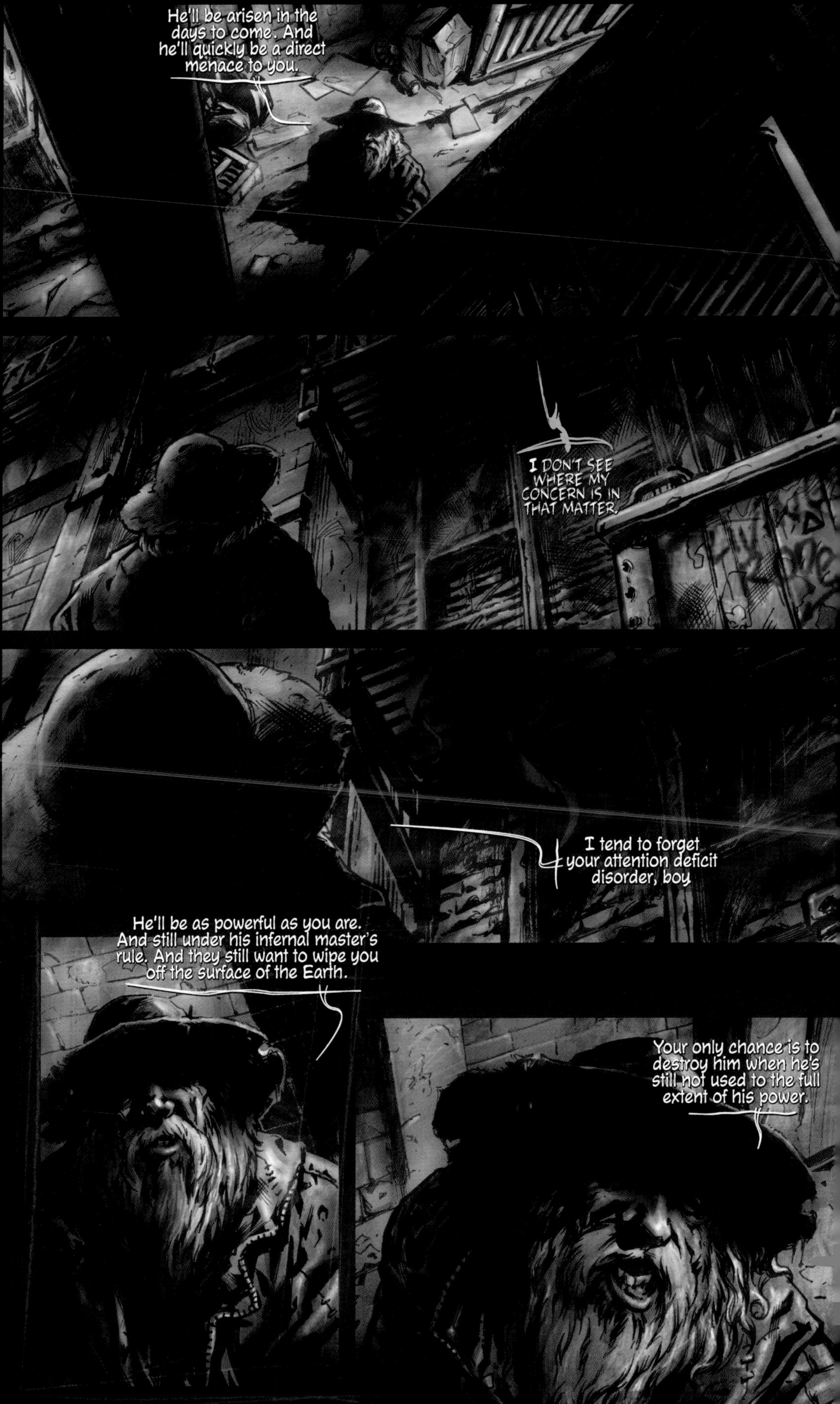
He'll be arisen in the days to come. And he'll quickly be a direct menace to you.
I DON'T SEE WHERE MY CONCERN IS IN THAT MATTER.
I tend to forget your attention deficit disorder, boy
He'll be as powerful as you are. And still under his infernal master's rule. And they still want to wipe you off the surface of the Earth.
Your only chance is to destroy him when he's still not used to the full extent of his power.

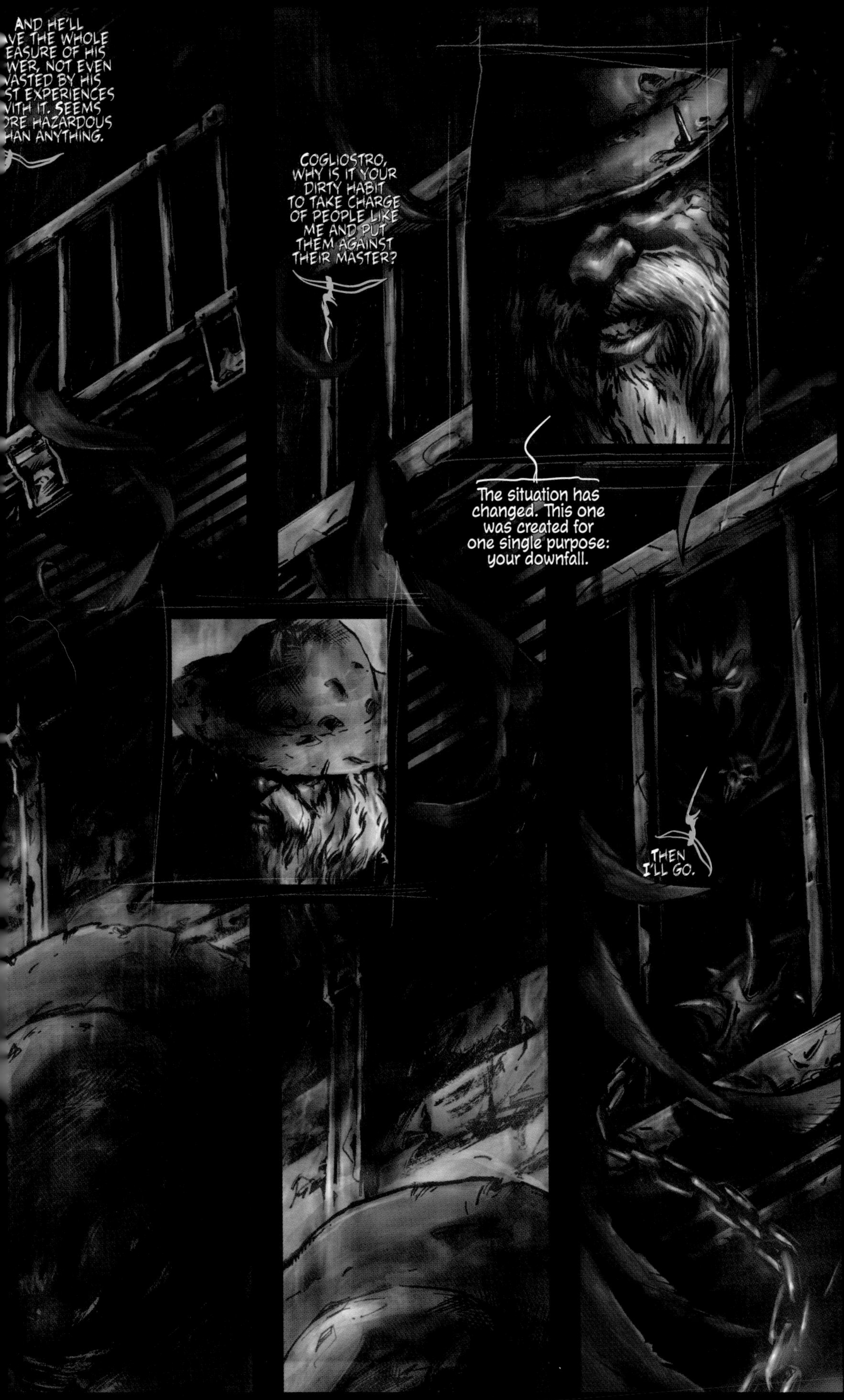
AND HE'LL
VE THE WHOLE
EASURE OF HIS
WER, NOT EVEN
VASTED BY HIS
ST EXPERIENCES
VITH IT. SEEMS
ORE HAZARDOUS
HAN ANYTHING.
COGLIOSTRO, WHY IS IT YOUR DIRTY HABIT TO TAKE CHARGE OF PEOPLE LIKE ME AND PUT THEM AGAINST THEIR MASTER?
The situation has changed. This one was created for one single purpose: your downfall.
THEN I'LL GO.

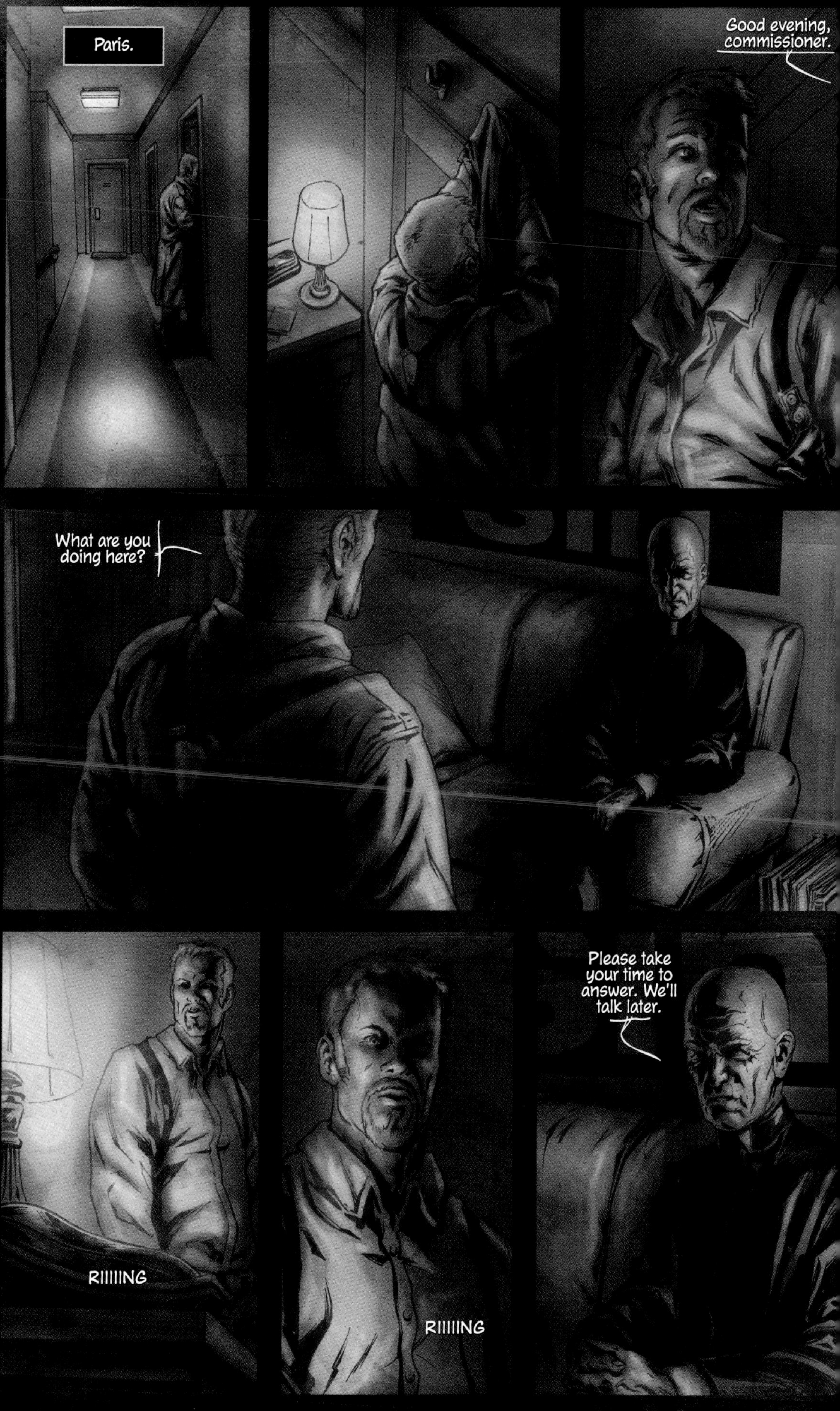
Paris.
Good evening, commissioner.
What are you doing here?
RIIIING
RIIIING
Please take your time to answer. We'll talk later.

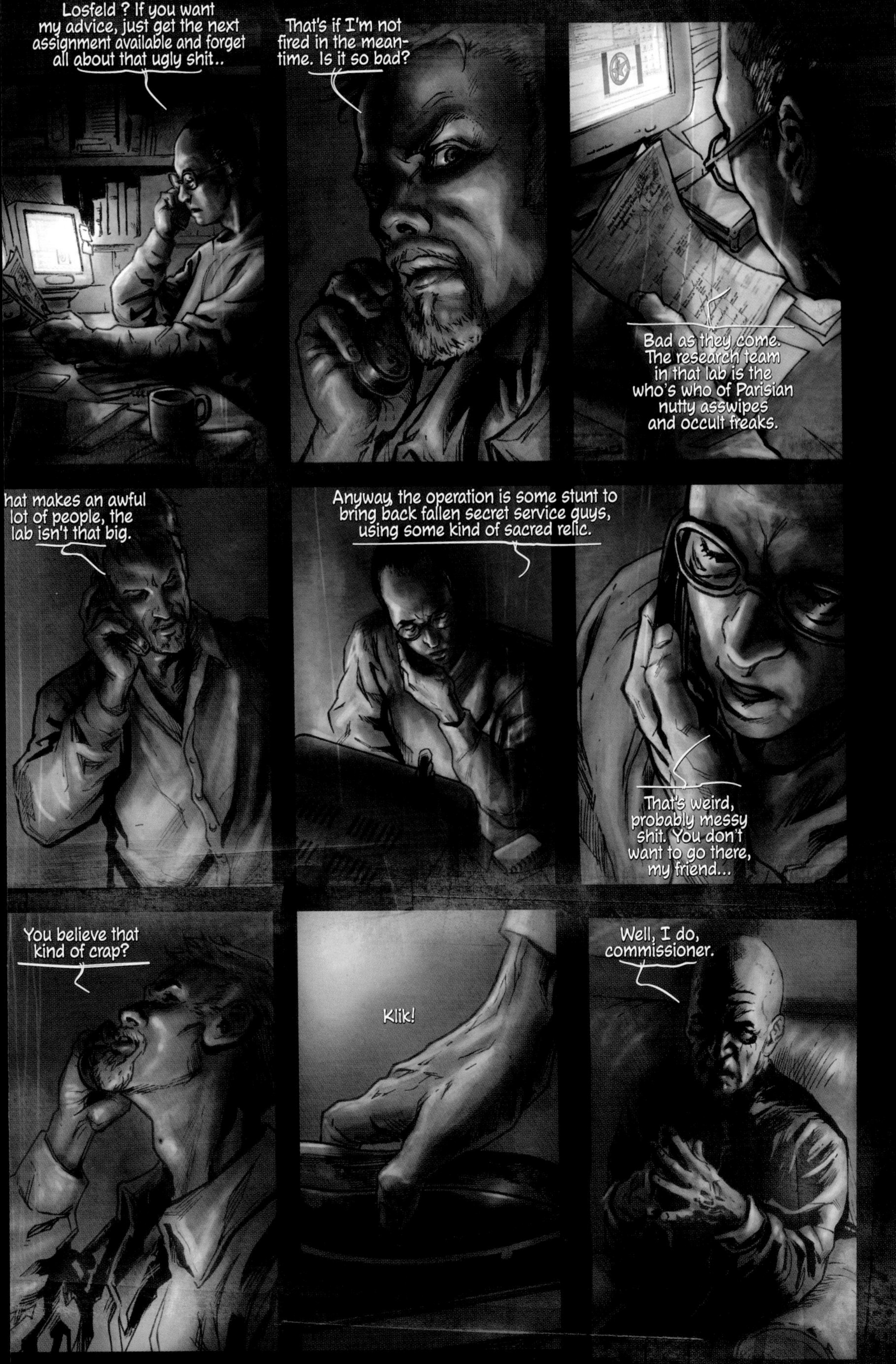
Losfeld ? If you want my advice, just get the next assignment available and forget all about that ugly shit..
That's if I'm not fired in the mean-time. Is it so bad?
Bad as they come. The research team in that lab is the who's who of Parisian nutty asswipes and occult freaks.
hat makes an awful lot of people, the lab isn't that big.
Anyway, the operation is some stunt to bring back fallen secret service guys, using some kind of sacred relic.
That's weird, probably messy shit. You don't want to go there, my friend...
You believe that kind of crap?
Klik!
Well, I do, commissioner.

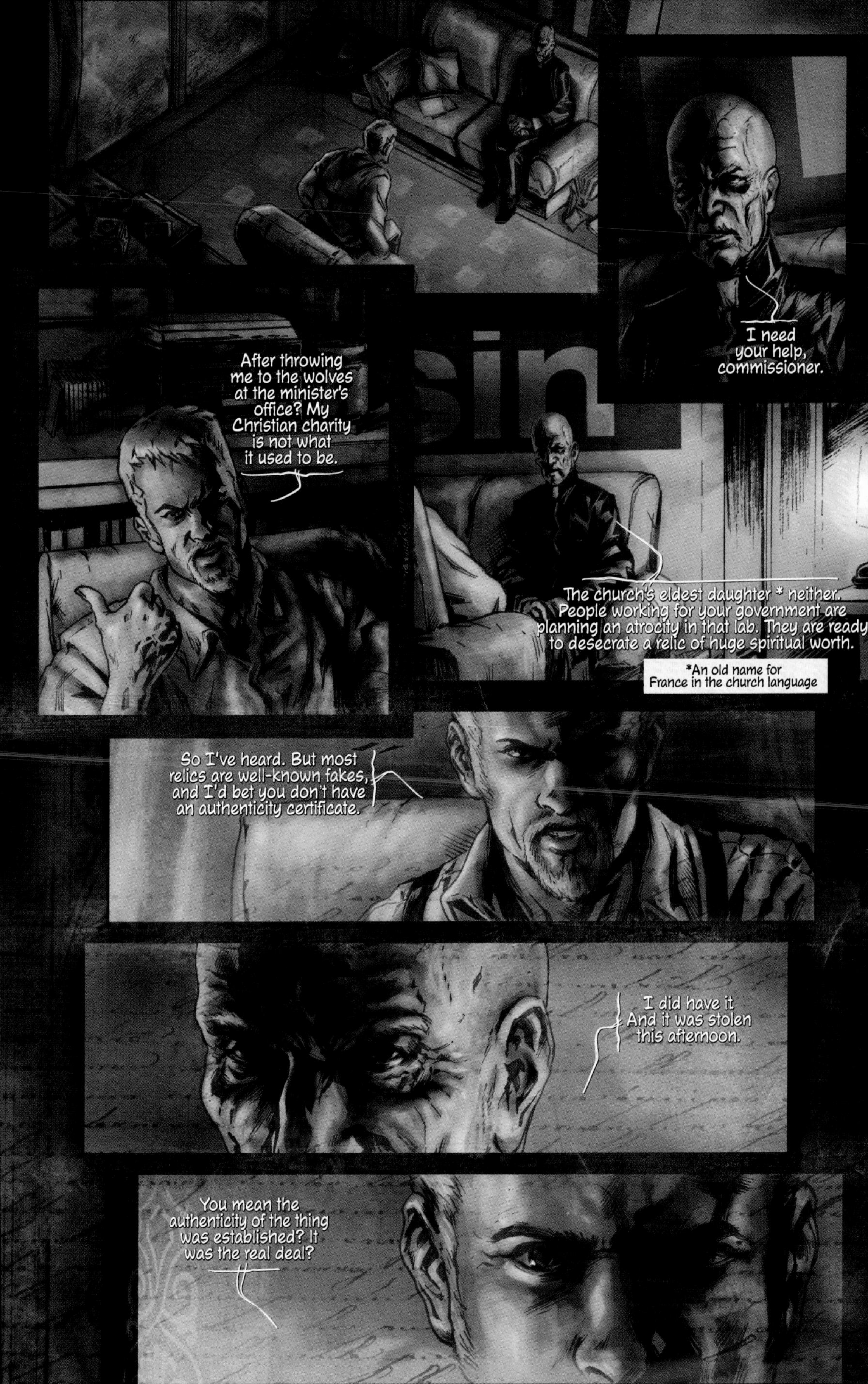
I need your help, commissioner.
After throwing me to the wolves at the minister's office? My Christian charity is not what it used to be.
The church's eldest daughter * neither. People working for your government are planning an atrocity in that lab. They are ready to desecrate a relic of huge spiritual worth.
*An old name for France in the church language
So I've heard. But most relics are well-known fakes, and I'd bet you don't have an authenticity certificate.
I did have it And it was stolen this afternoon.
You mean the authenticity of the thing was established? It was the real deal?

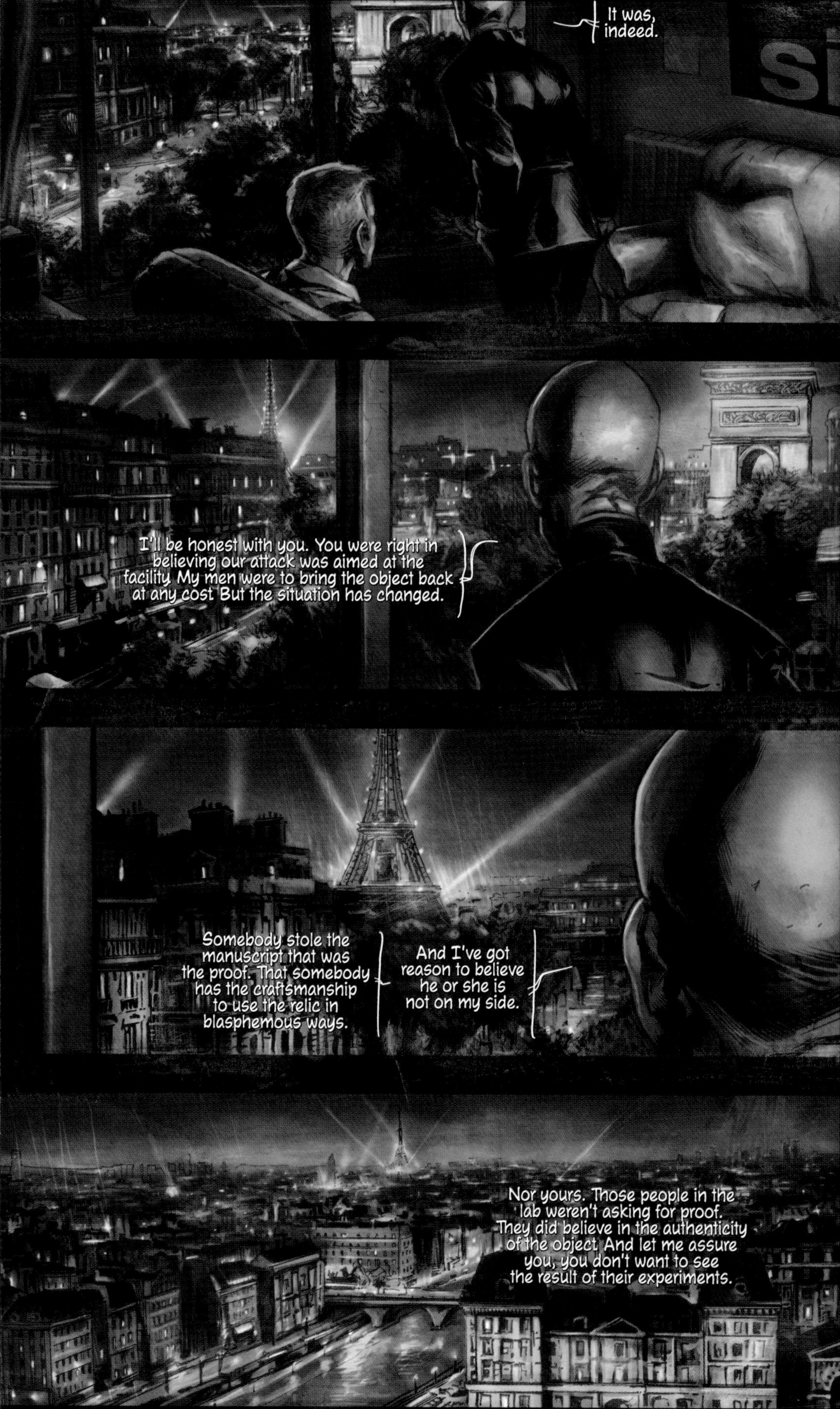
It was, indeed.
I'll be honest with you. You were right in believing our attack was aimed at the facility. My men were to bring the object back at any cost. But the situation has changed.
Somebody stole the manuscript that was the proof. That somebody has the craftsmanship to use the relic in blasphemous ways.
And I've got reason to believe he or she is not on my side.
Nor yours. Those people in the lab weren't asking for proof. They did believe in the authenticity of the object. And let me assure you, you don't want to see the result of their experiments.

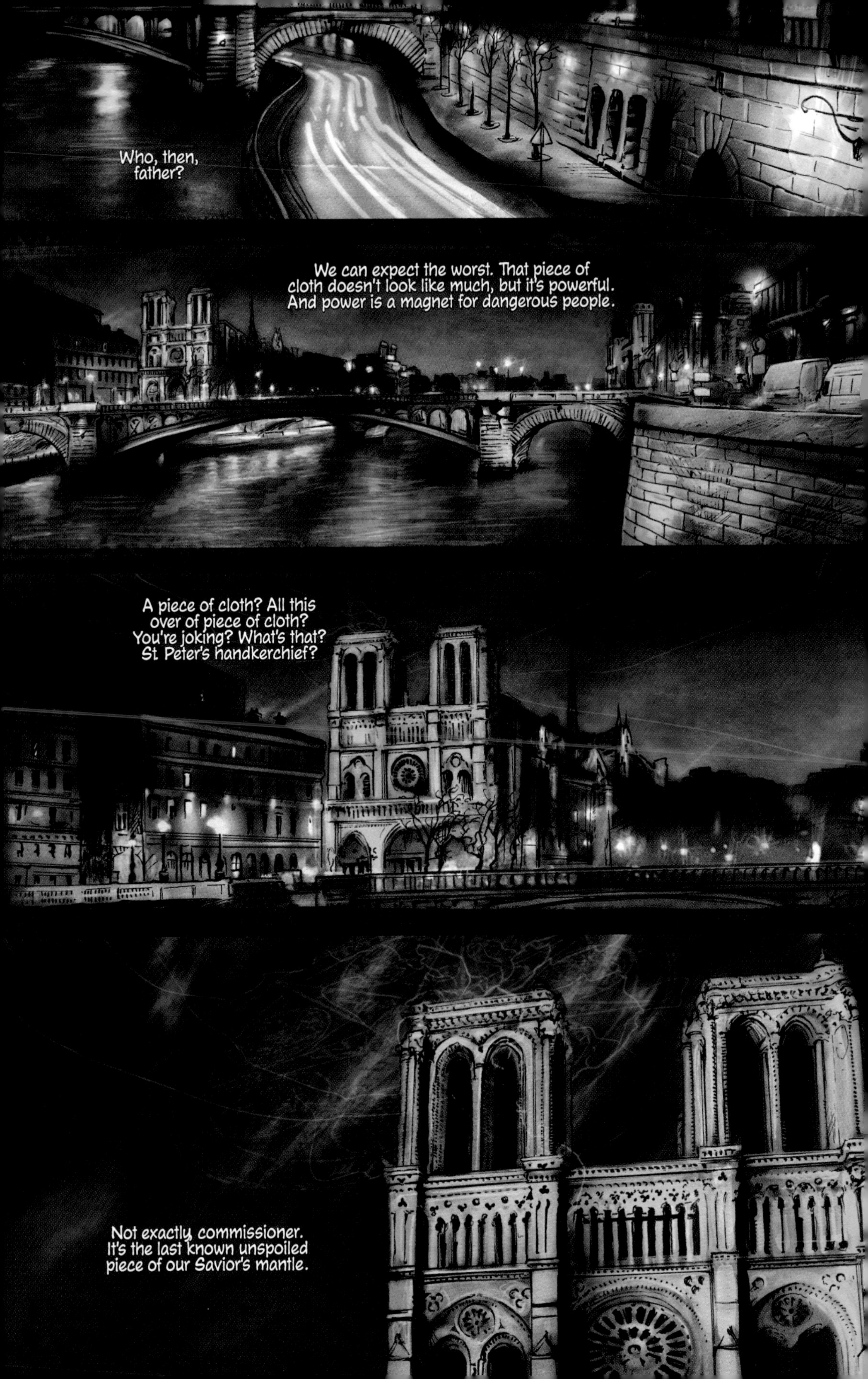
Who, then, father?
We can expect the worst. That piece of cloth doesn't look like much, but it's powerful. And power is a magnet for dangerous people.
A piece of cloth? All this over of piece of cloth? You're joking? What's that? St. Peter's handkerchief?
Not exactly commissioner. It's the last known unspoiled piece of our Savior's mantle.

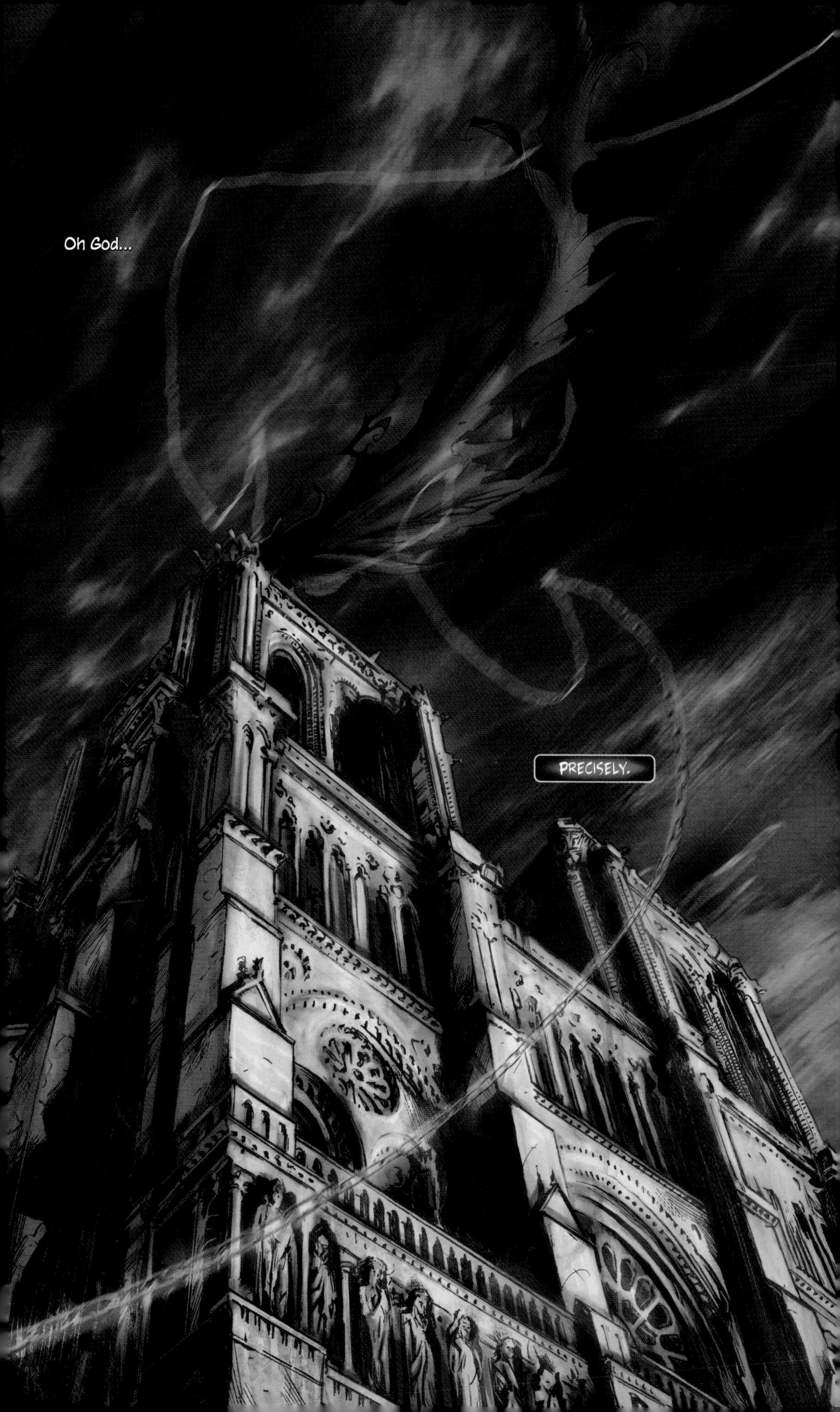

Oh God...
PRECISELY.

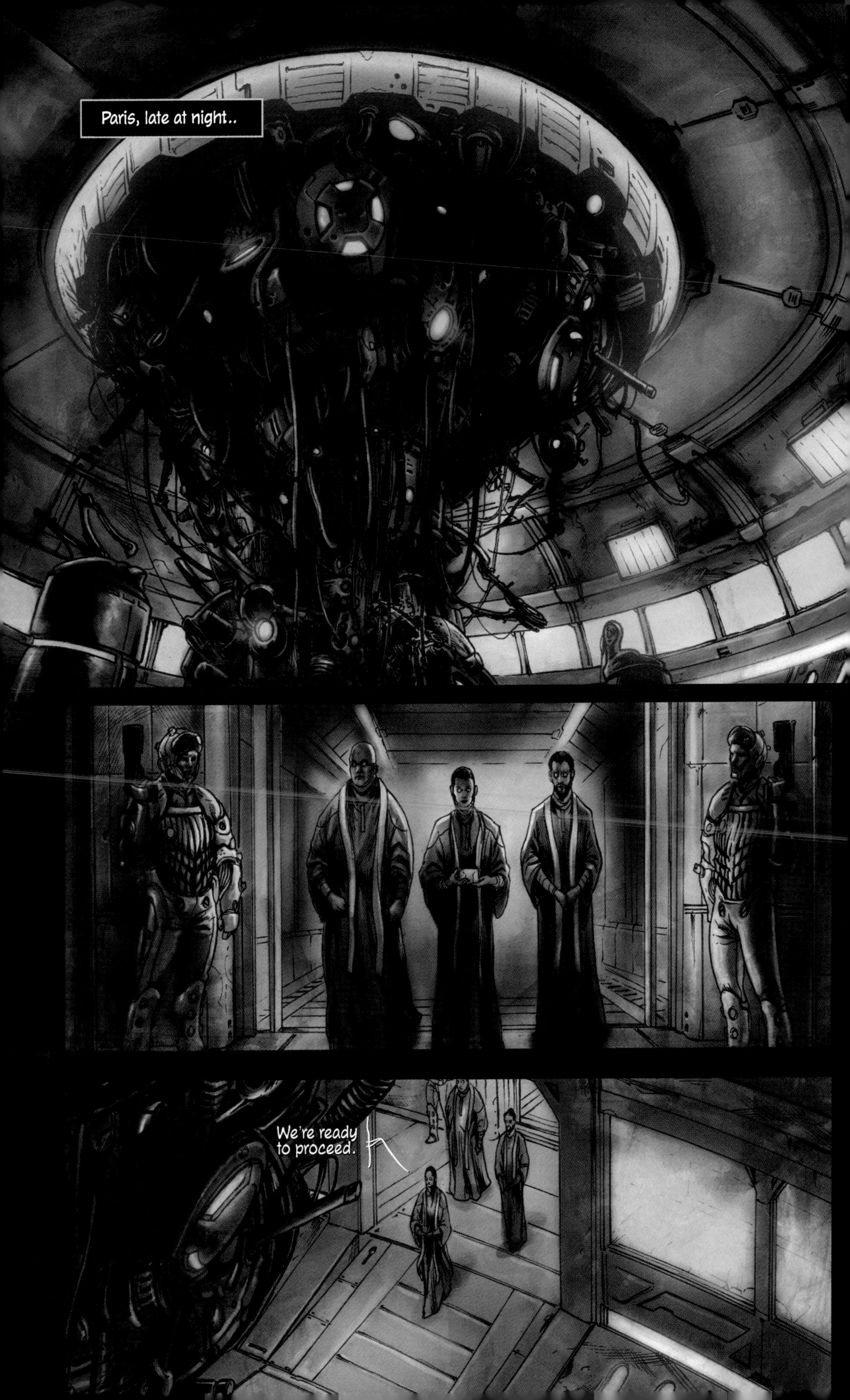
Paris, late at night..
We're ready to proceed.

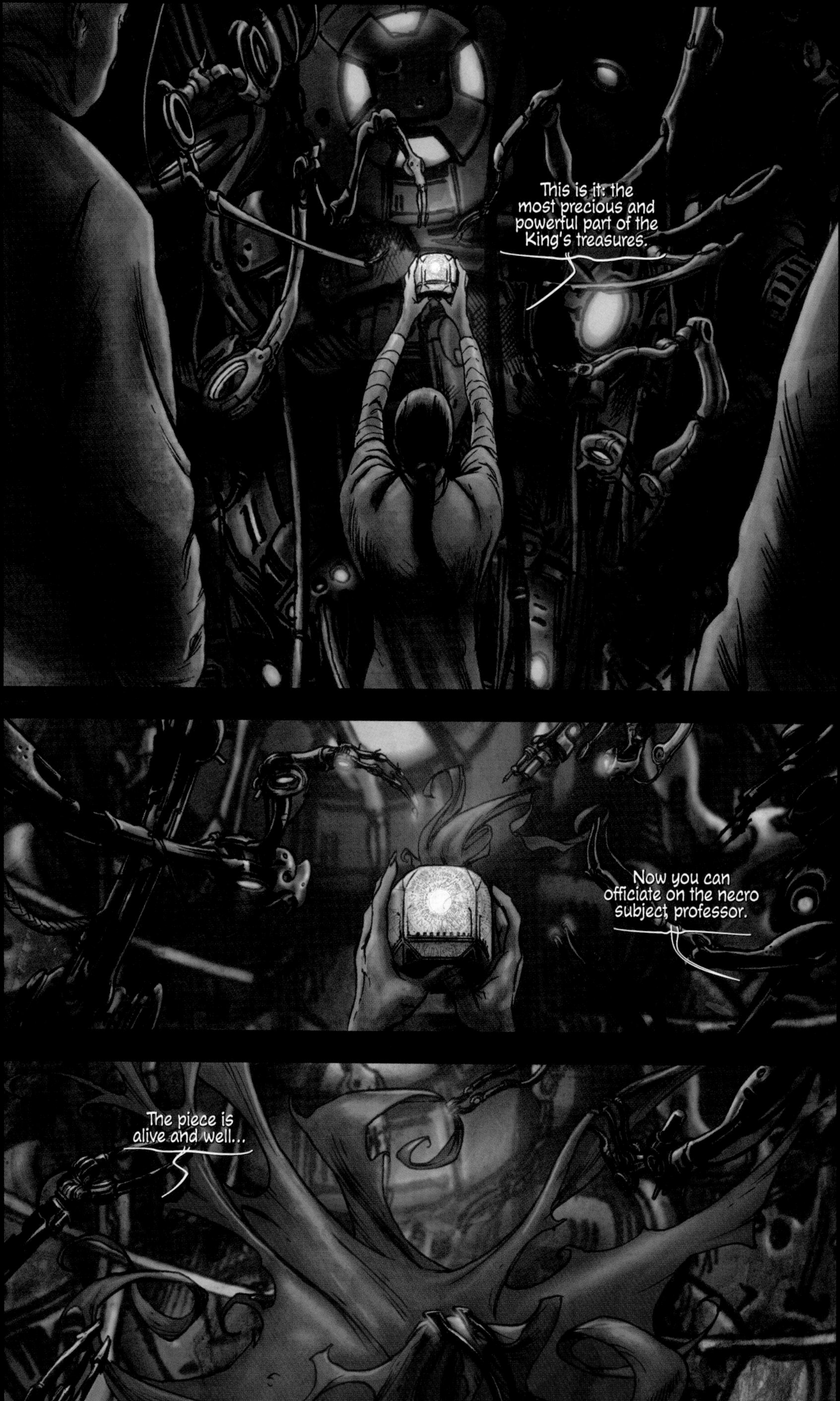
This is it: the most precious and powerful part of the King's treasures.
Now you can officiate on the necro subject, professor.
The piece is alive and well...

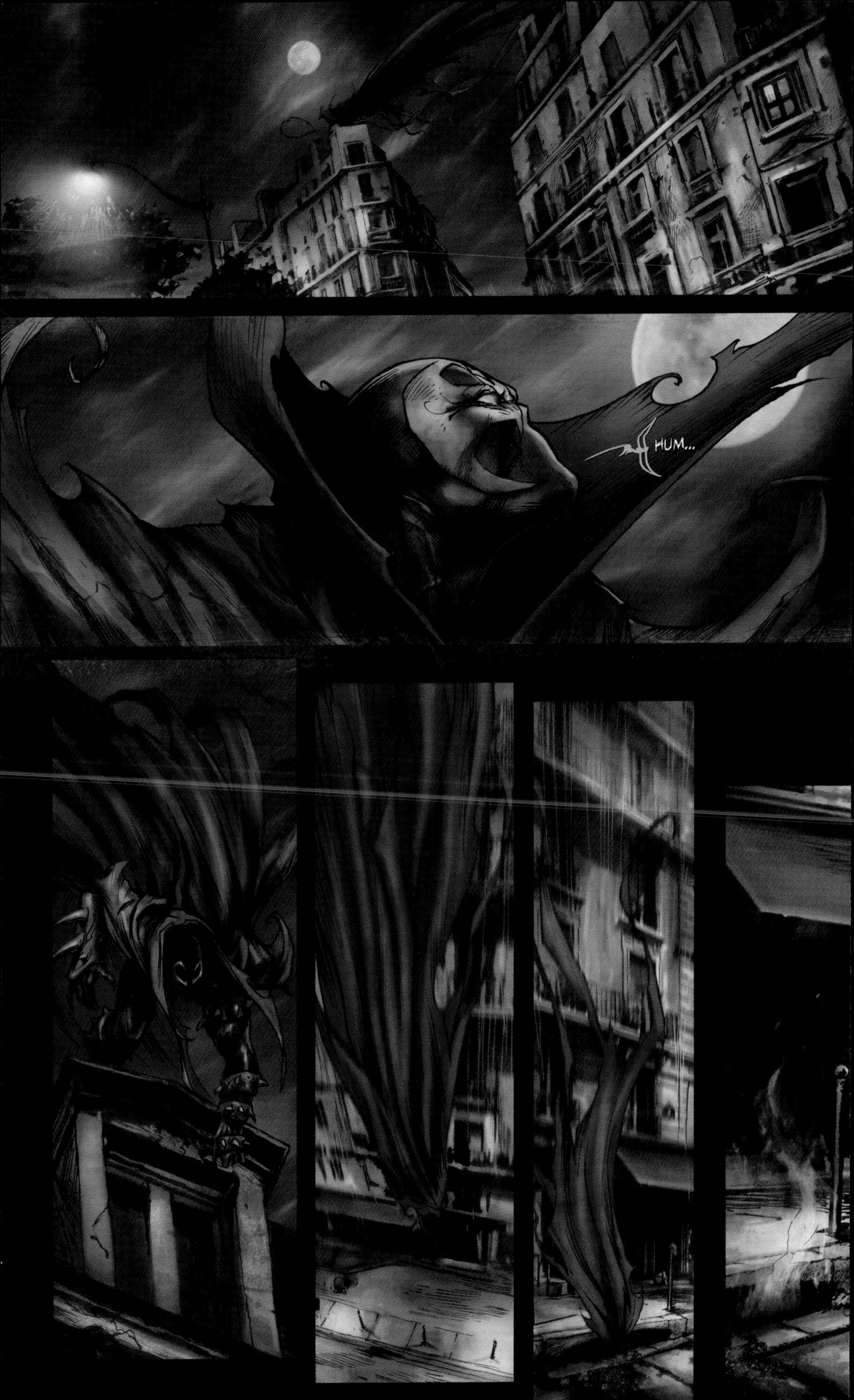
HUM...

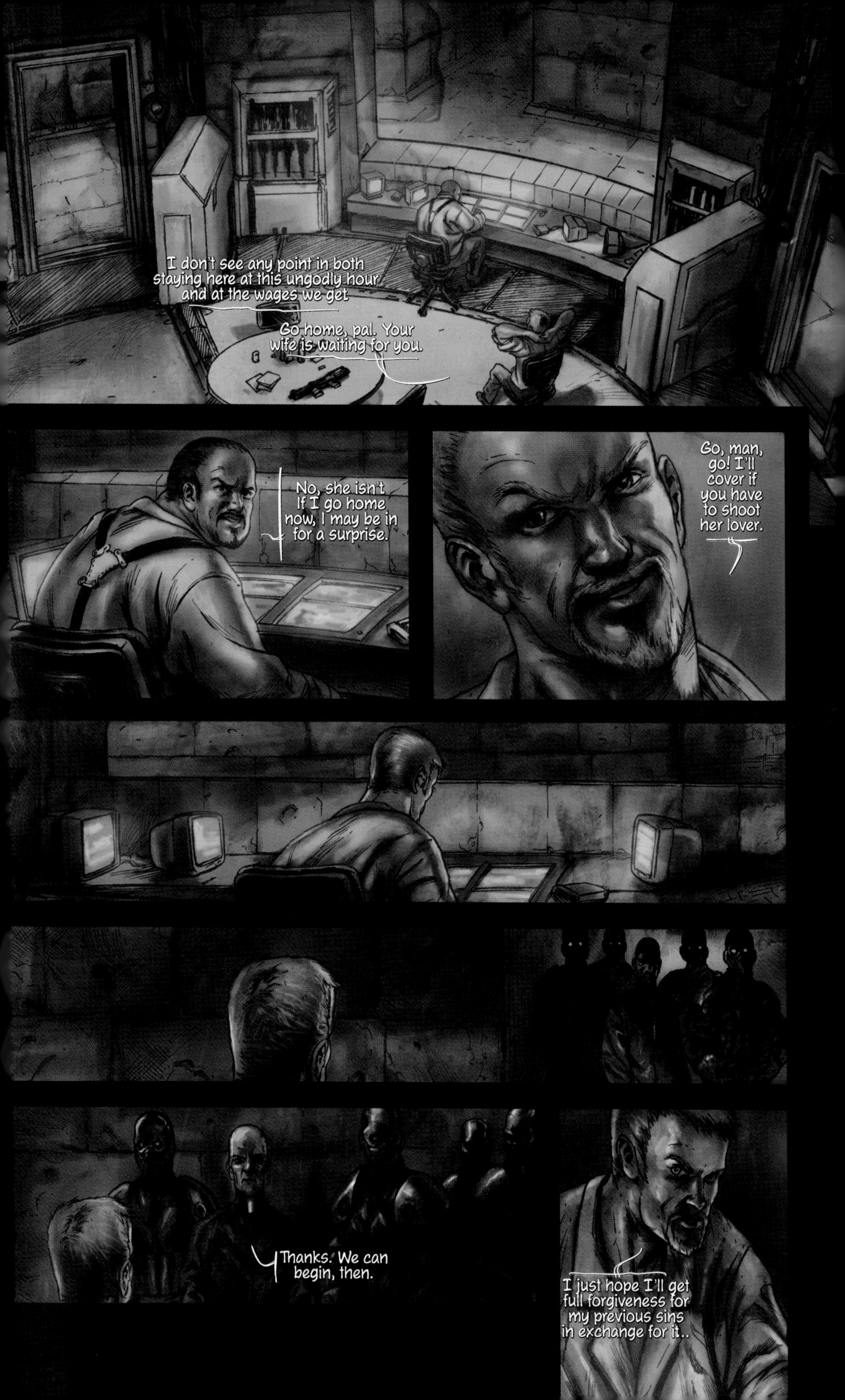
I don't see any point in both staying here at this ungodly hour and at the wages we get
Go home, pal. Your wife is waiting for you.
No, she isn't. If I go home now, I may be in for a surprise.
Go, man, go! I'll cover if you have to shoot her lover.
Thanks. We can begin, then.
I just hope I'll get full forgiveness for my previous sins in exchange for it..

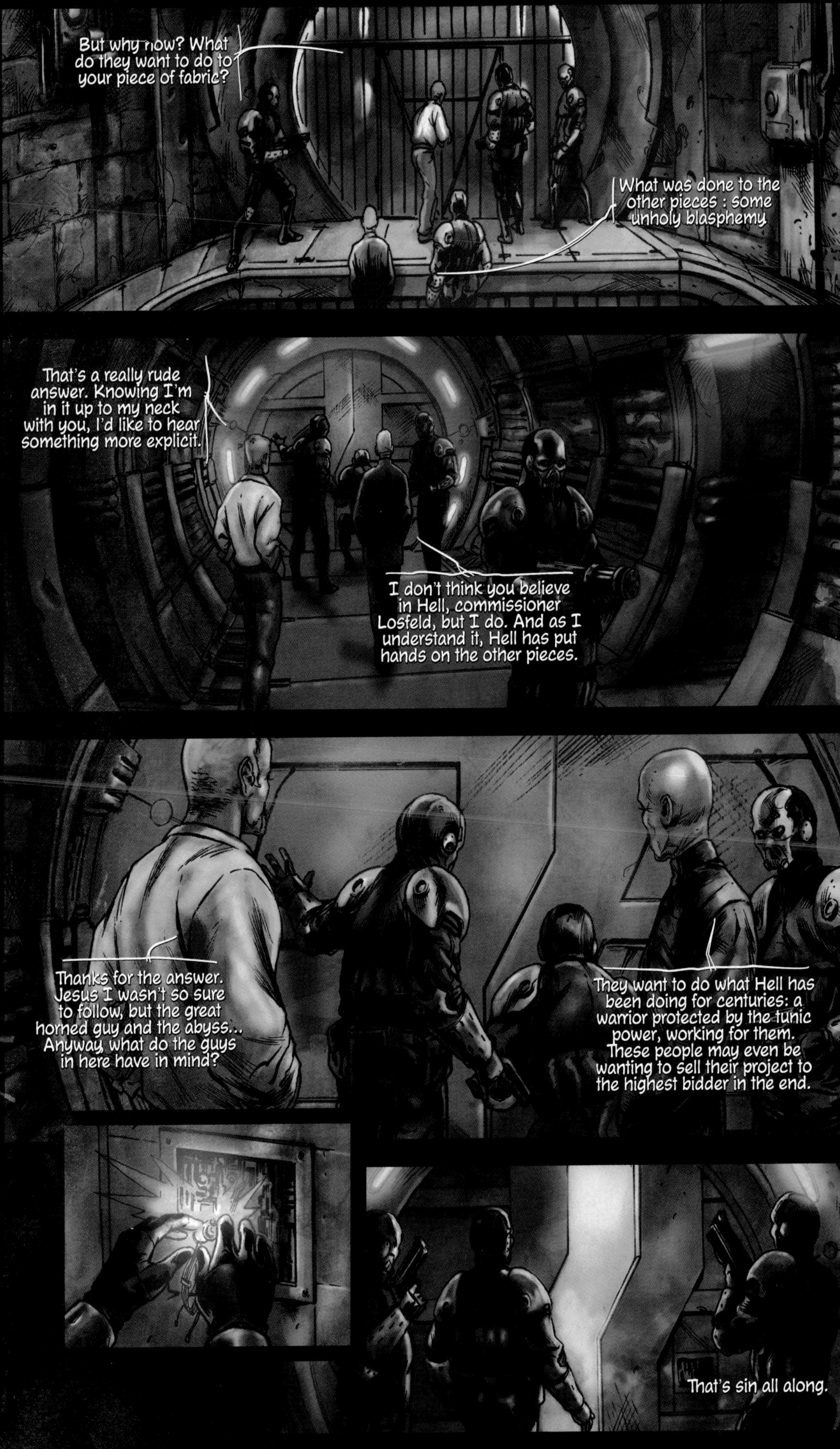

But why now? What do they want to do to your piece of fabric?
What was done to the other pieces : some unholy blasphemy
That's a really rude answer. Knowing I'm in it up to my neck with you, I'd like to hear something more explicit.
I don't think you believe in Hell, commissioner Losfeld, but I do. And as I understand it, Hell has put hands on the other pieces.
Thanks for the answer. Jesus I wasn't so sure to follow, but the great horned guy and the abyss... Anyway, what do the guys in here have in mind?
They want to do what Hell has been doing for centuries: a warrior protected by the tunic power, working for them. These people may even be wanting to sell their project to the highest bidder in the end.
That's sin all along.

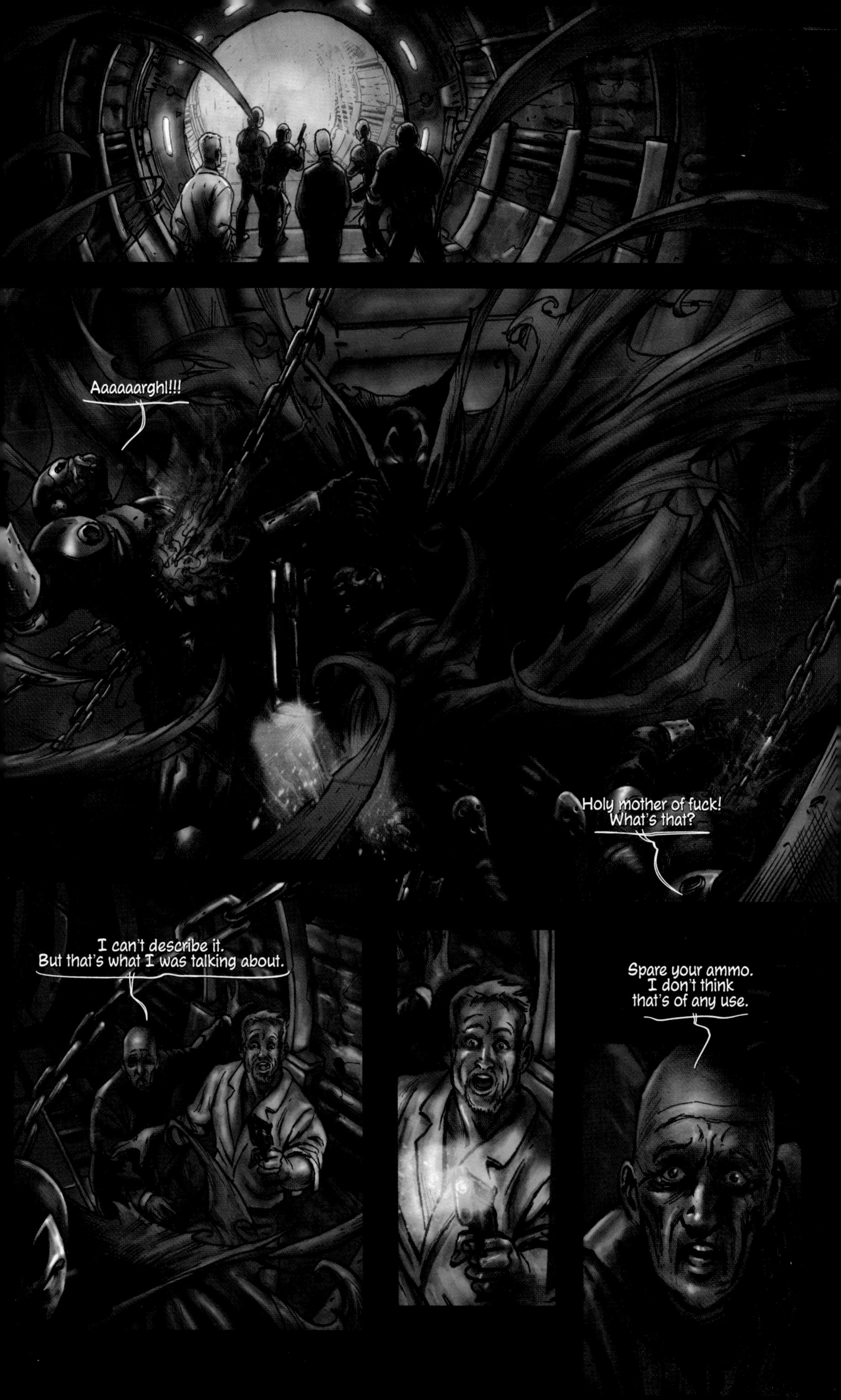
Aaaaaarghl!!!
Holy mother of fuck! What's that?
I can't describe it. But that's what I was talking about.
Spare your ammo. I don't think that's of any use.

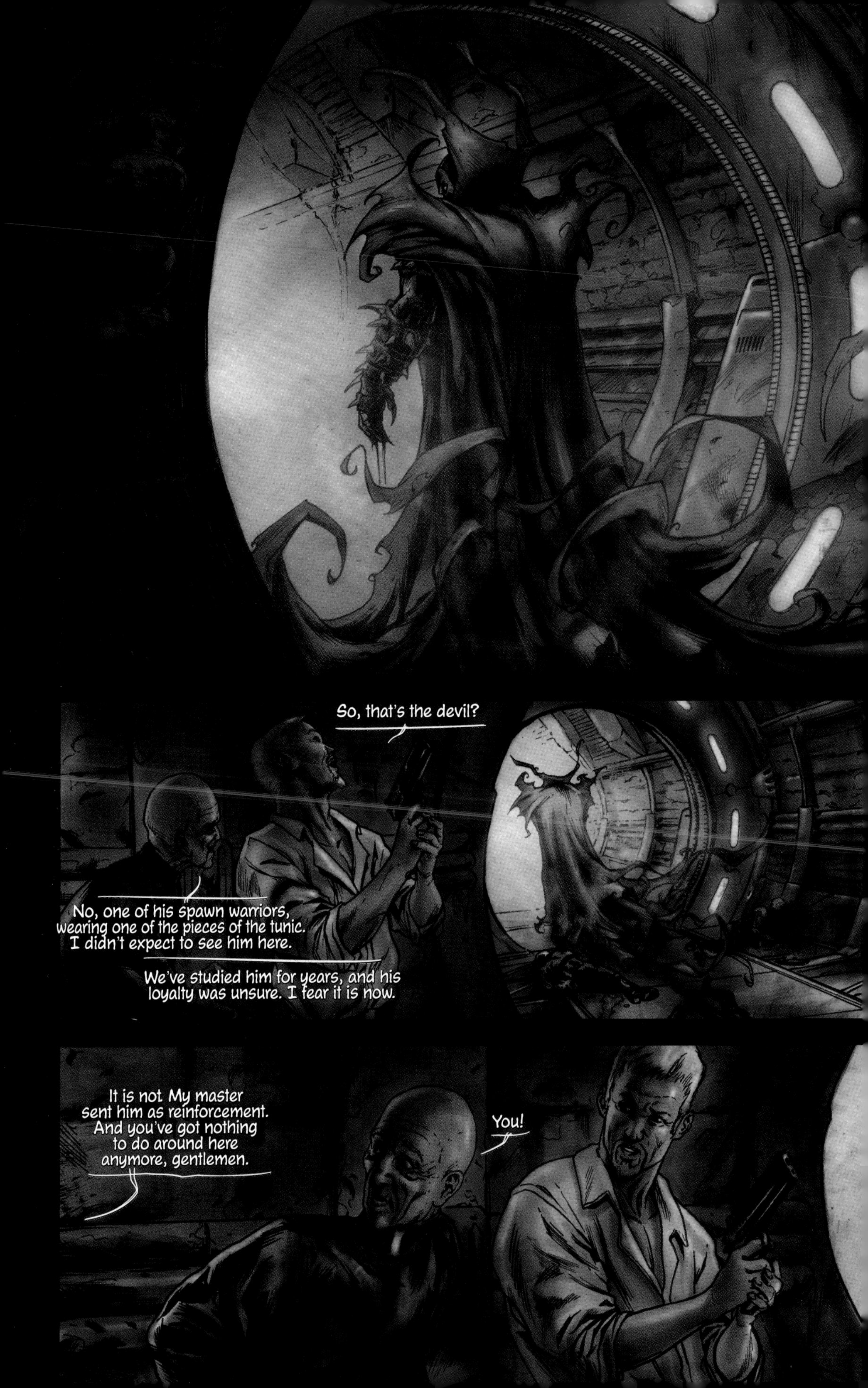
So, that's the devil?
No, one of his spawn warriors, wearing one of the pieces of the tunic. I didn't expect to see him here.
We've studied him for years, and his loyalty was unsure. I fear it is now.
It is not. My master sent him as reinforcement. And you've got nothing to do around here anymore, gentlemen.
You!

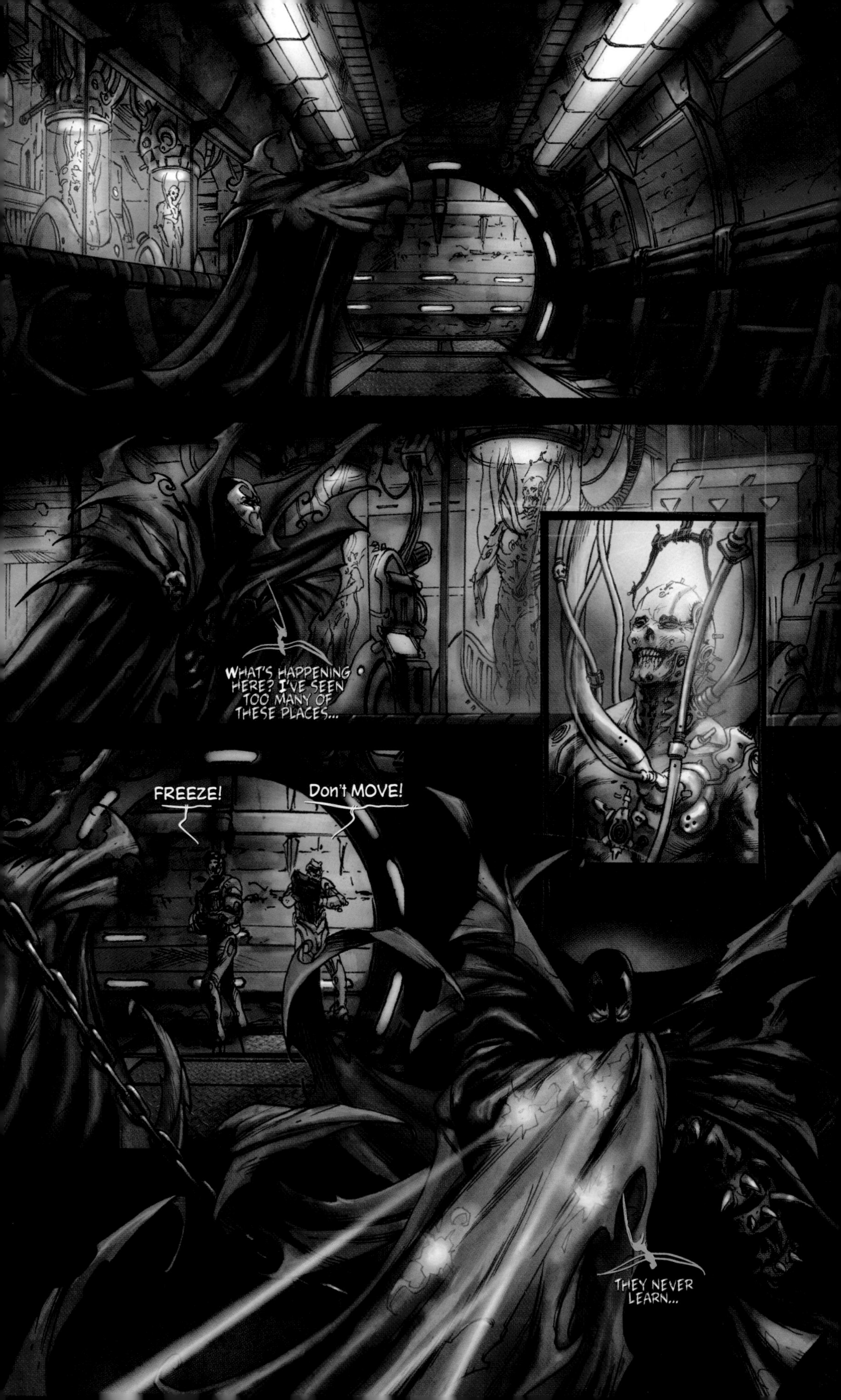
WHAT'S HAPPENING HERE? I'VE SEEN TOO MANY OF THESE PLACES...
FREEZE!
Don't MOVE!
THEY NEVER LEARN...

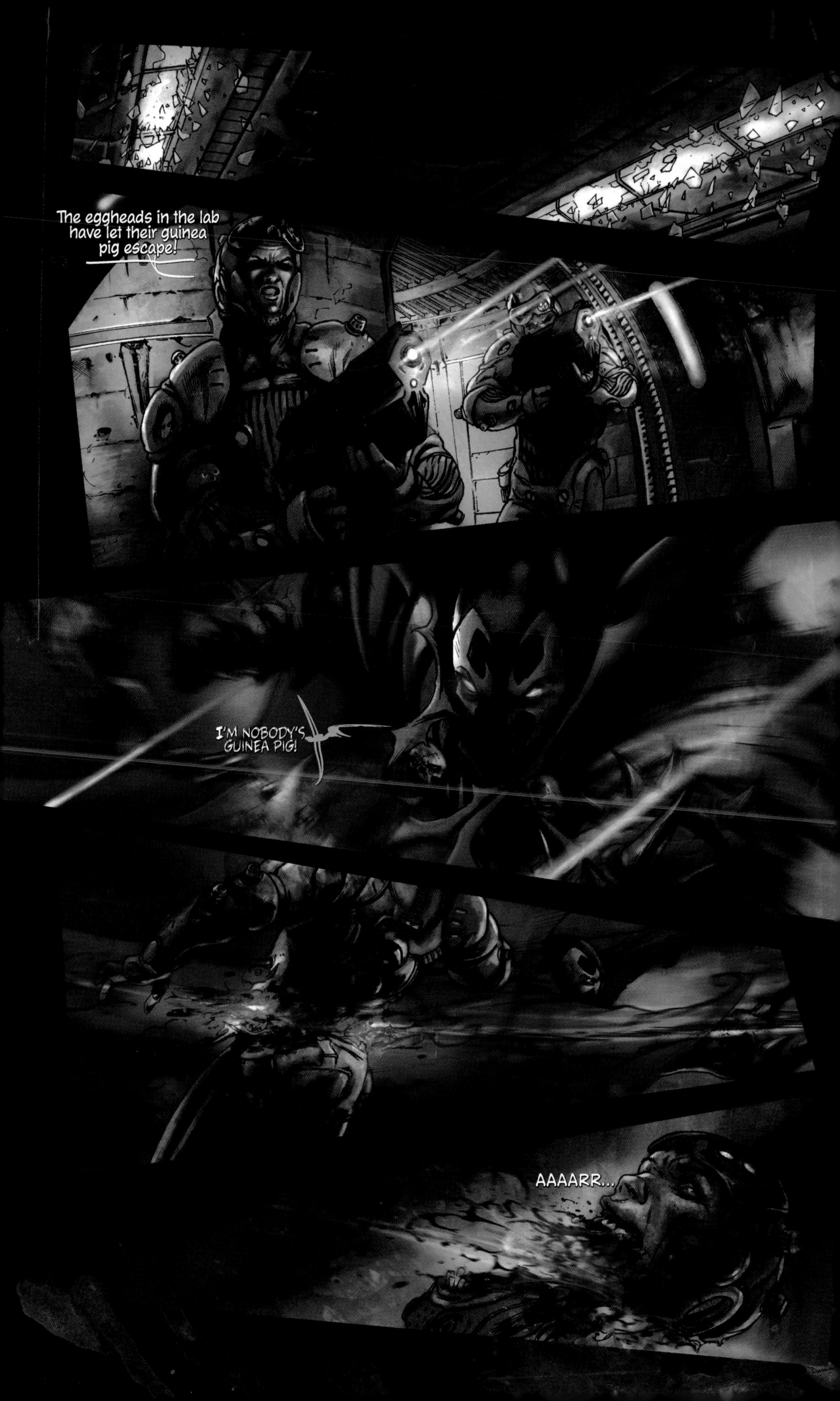

The eggheads in the lab have let their guinea pig escape!
I'M NOBODY'S GUINEA PIG!
AAAARR...

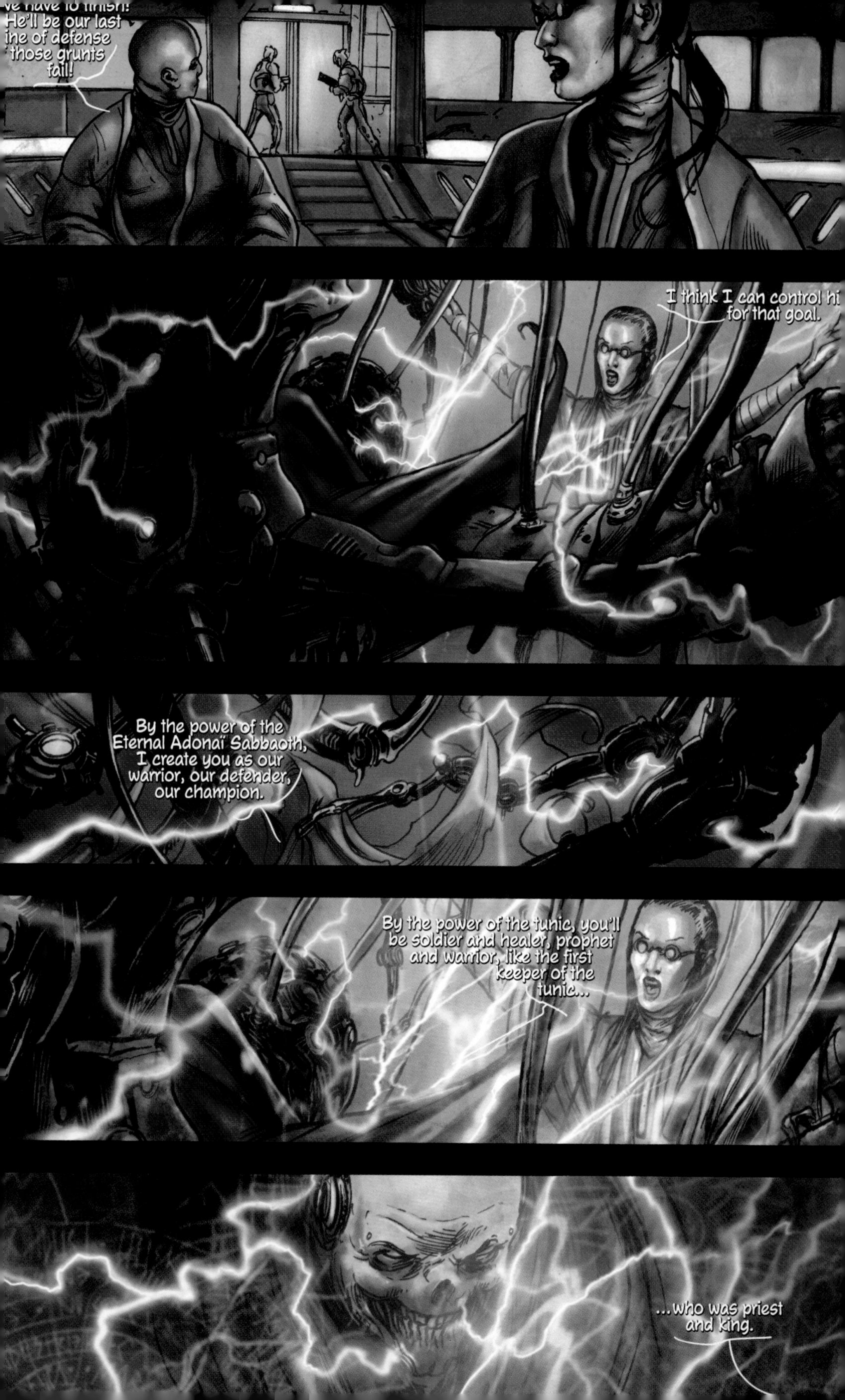

ve have to finish! He'll be our last ine of defense those grunts fail!
I think I can control hi for that goal.
By the power of the Eternal Adonaï Sabbaoth, I create you as our warrior, our defender, our champion.
By the power of the tunic, you'll be soldier and healer, prophet and warrior, like the first keeper of the tunic...
...who was priest and king.

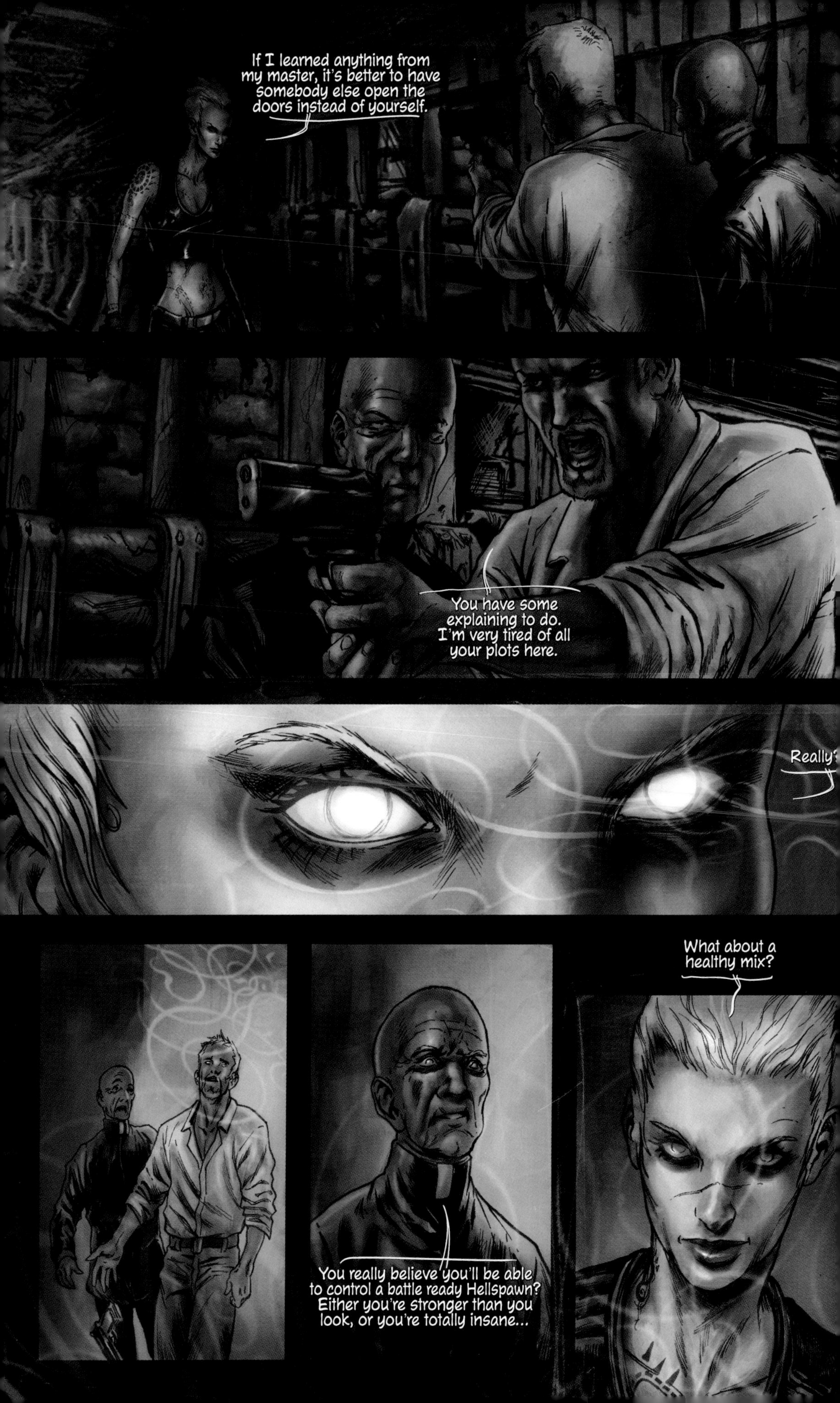

If I learned anything from my master, it's better to have somebody else open the doors instead of yourself.
You have some explaining to do. I'm very tired of all your plots here.
Really?
You really believe you'll be able to control a battle ready Hellspawn? Either you're stronger than you look, or you're totally insane...
What about a healthy mix?

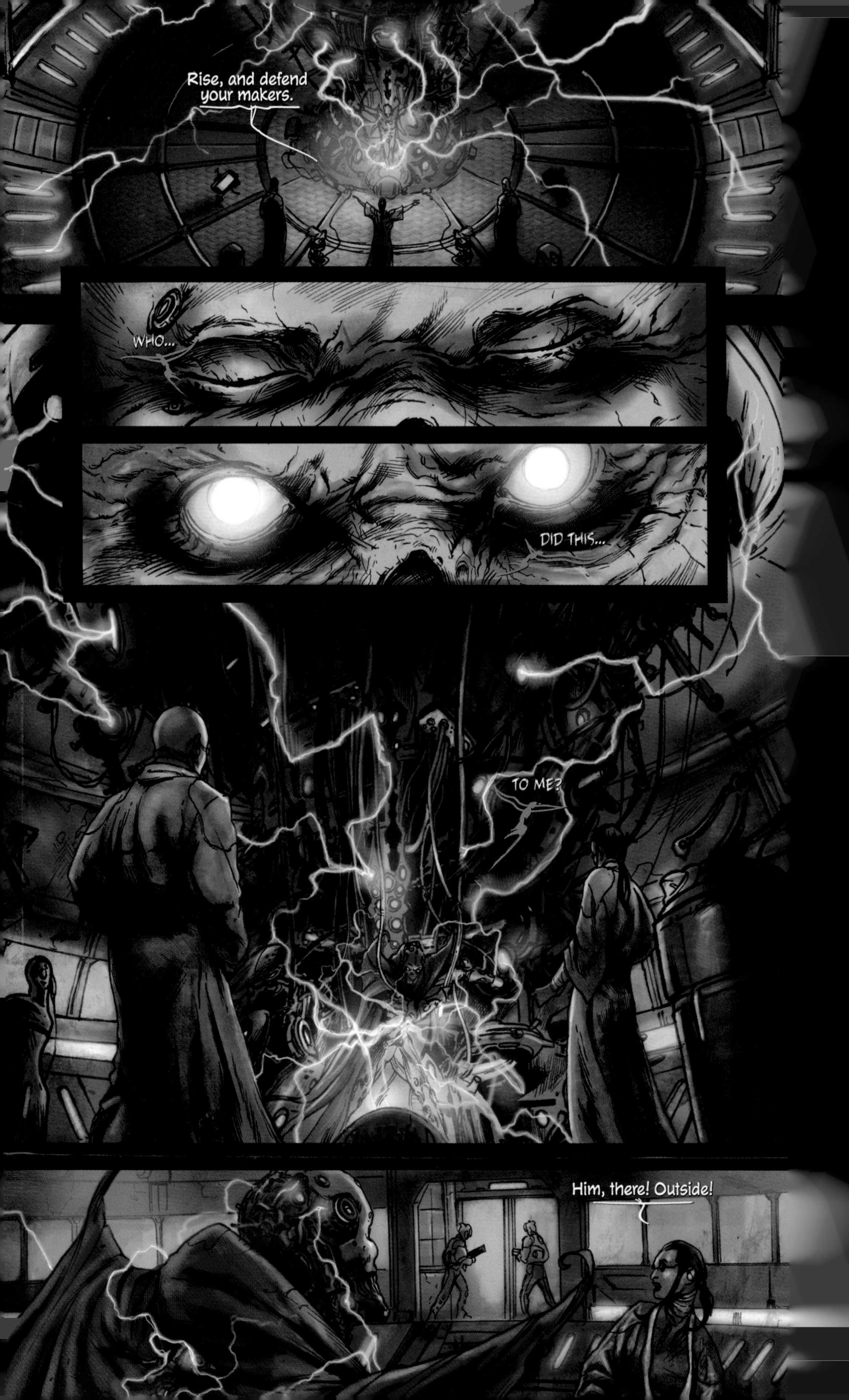
Rise, and defend your makers.
WHO...
DID THIS...
TO ME?
Him, there! Outside!

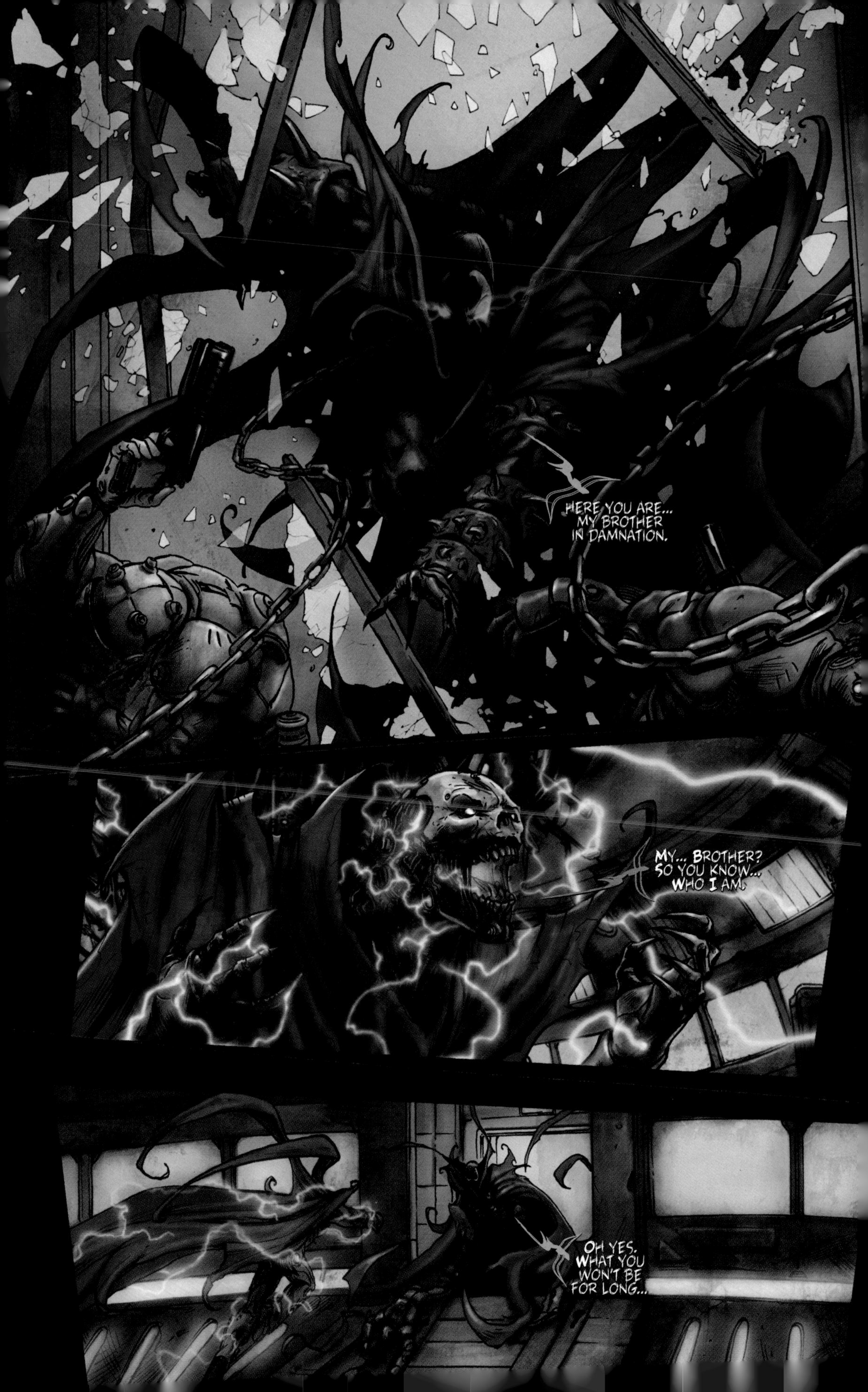
HERE YOU ARE... MY BROTHER IN DAMNATION.
MY... BROTHER? SO YOU KNOW... WHO I AM.
OH YES. WHAT YOU WON'T BE FOR LONG...

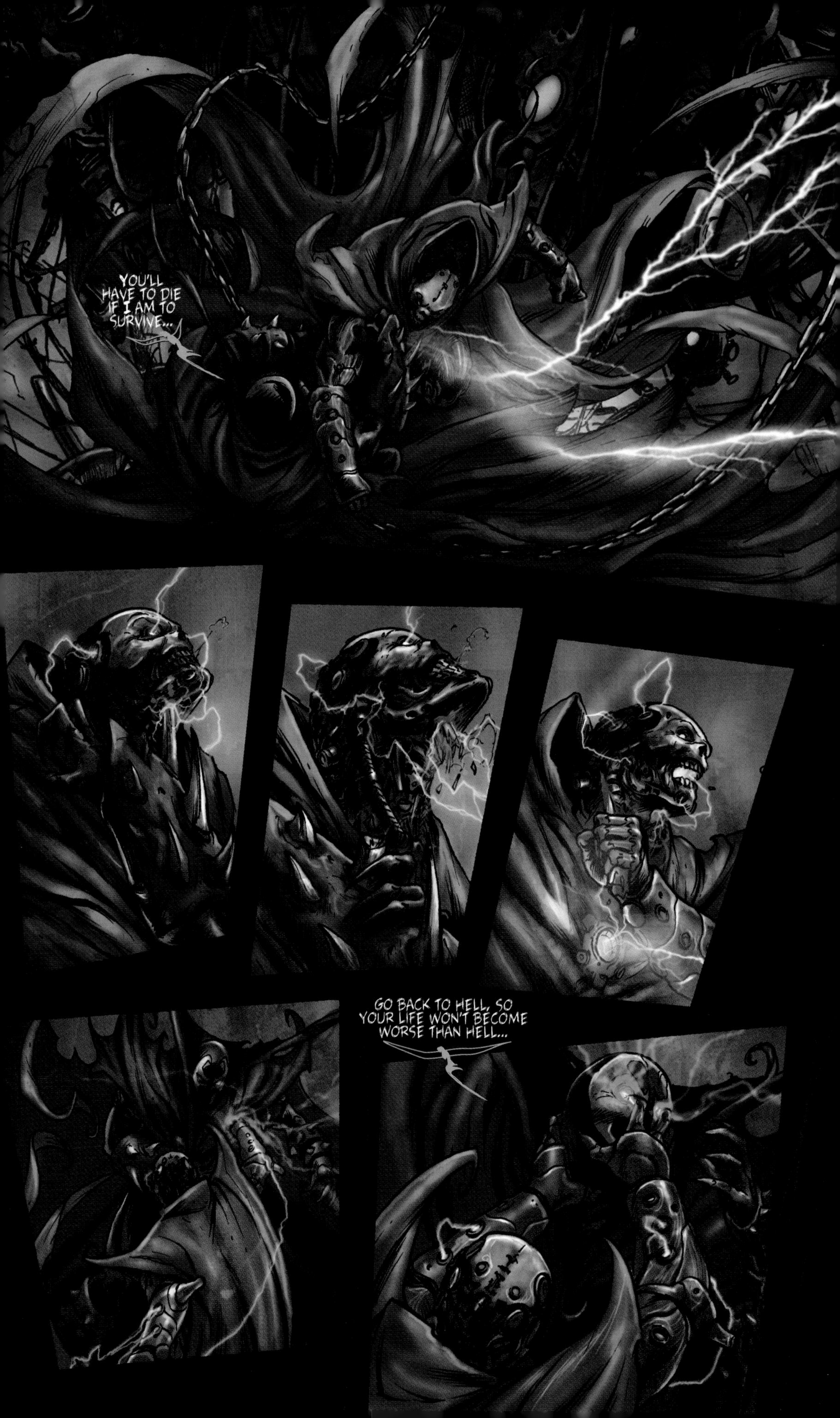
YOU'LL HAVE TO DIE IF I AM TO SURVIVE...
GO BACK TO HELL, SO YOUR LIFE WON'T BECOME WORSE THAN HELL...

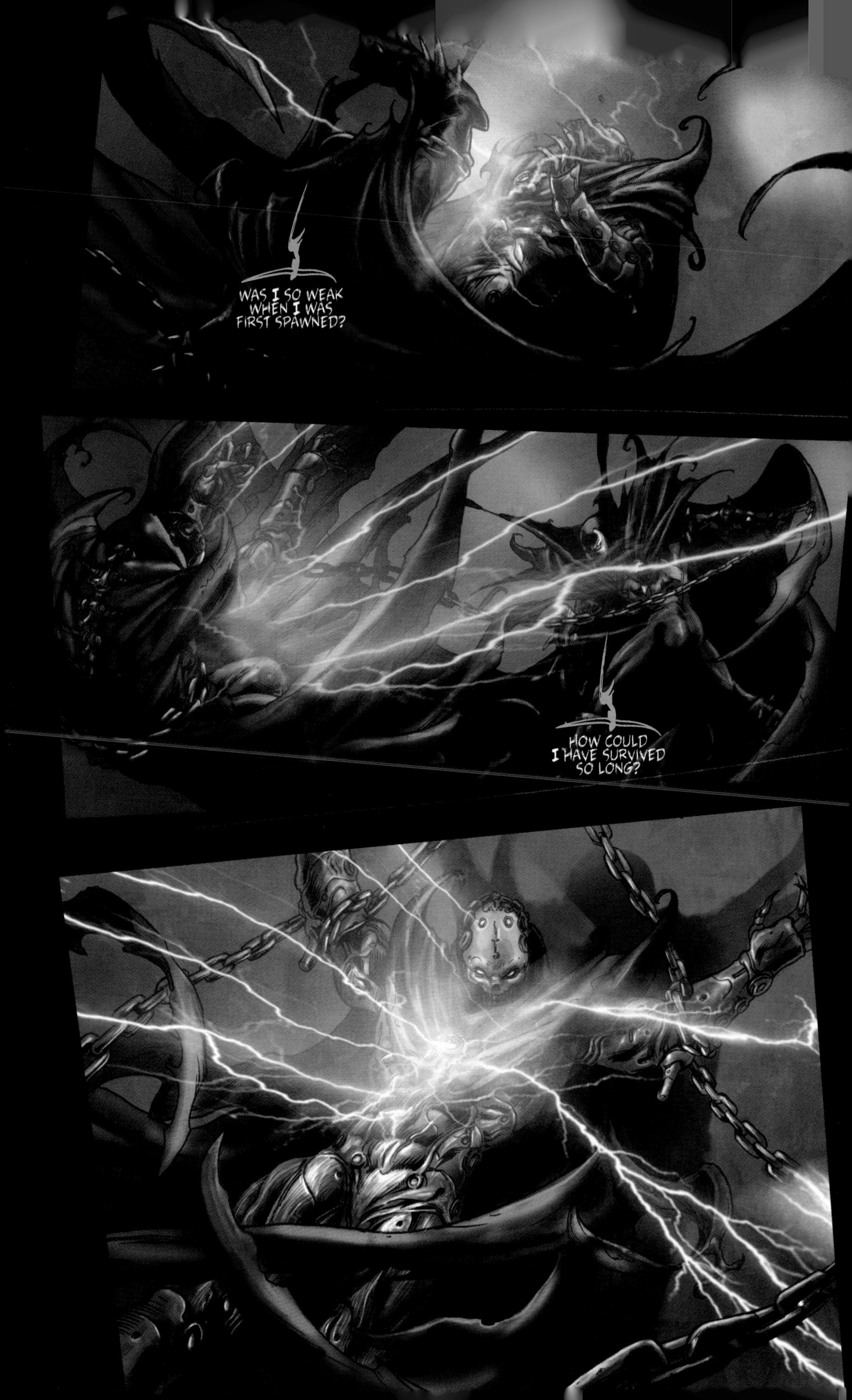
WAS I SO WEAK WHEN I WAS FIRST SPAWNED?
HOW COULD I HAVE SURVIVED SO LONG?

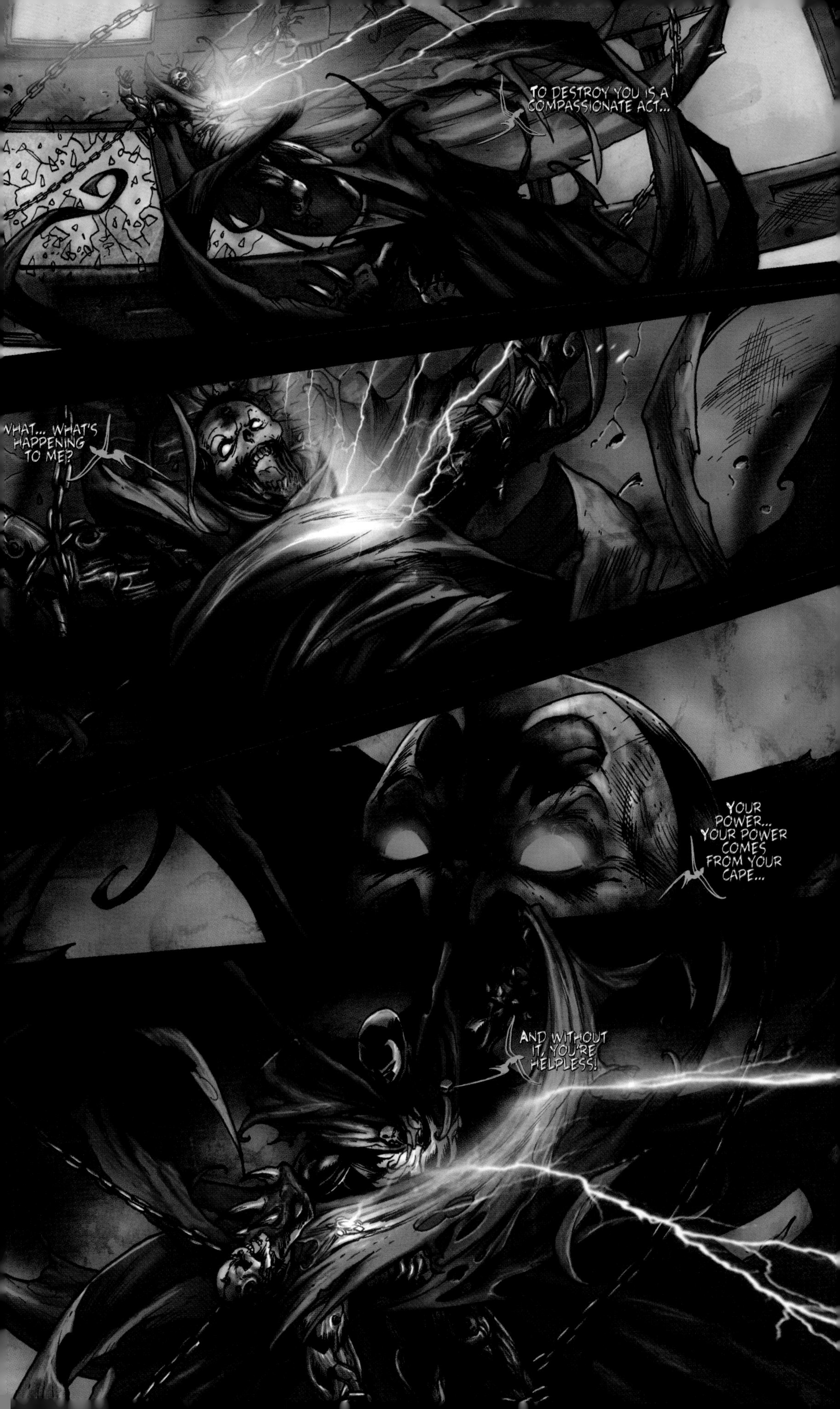

TO DESTROY YOU IS A COMPASSIONATE ACT...
WHAT... WHAT'S HAPPENING TO ME?
YOUR POWER... YOUR POWER COMES FROM YOUR CAPE...
AND WITHOUT IT, YOU'RE HELPLESS!

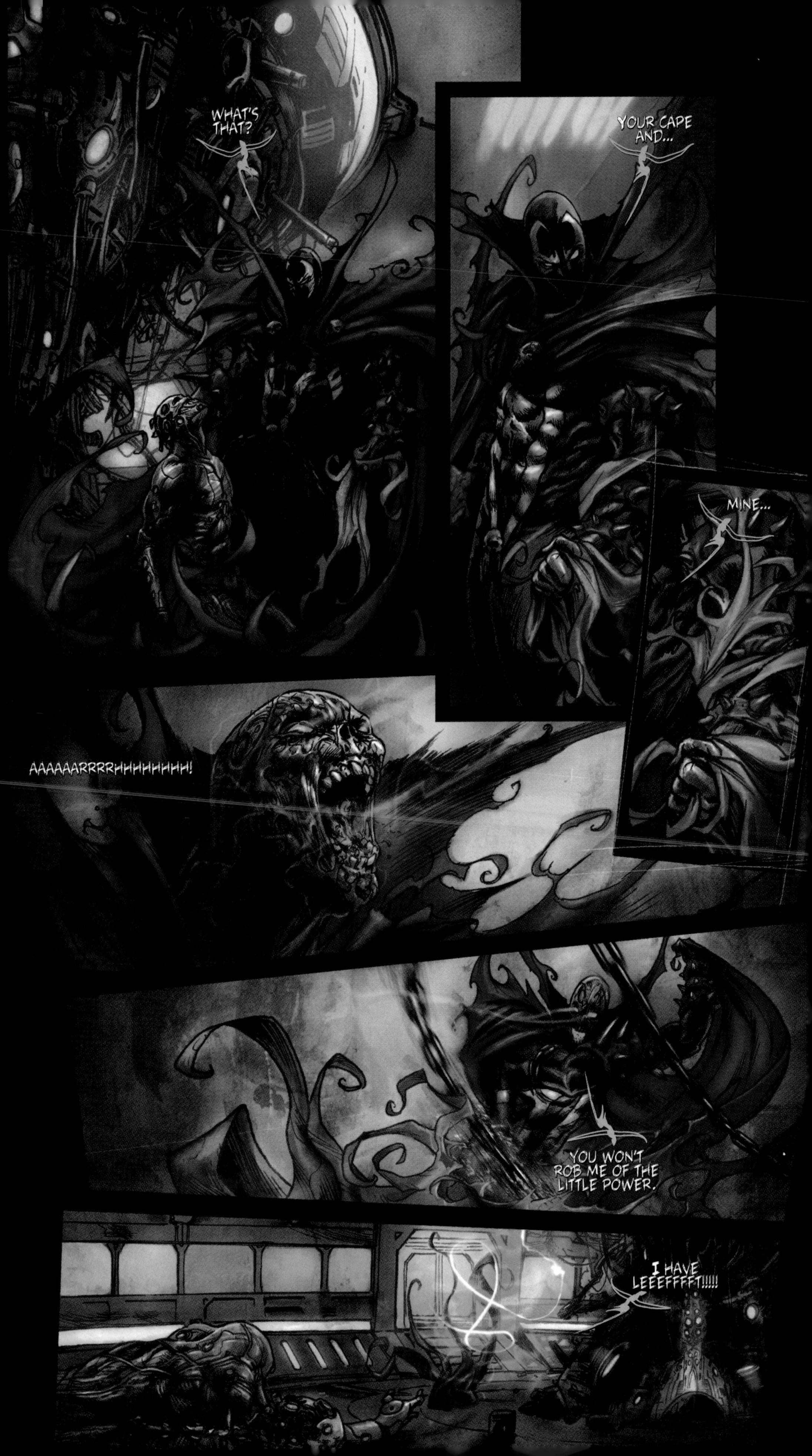
WHAT'S THAT?
YOUR CAPE AND...
MINE...
AAAAAARRRRHHHHHHHHH!
YOU WON'T ROB ME OF THE LITTLE POWER.
I HAVE LEEEFFFFFT!!!!!

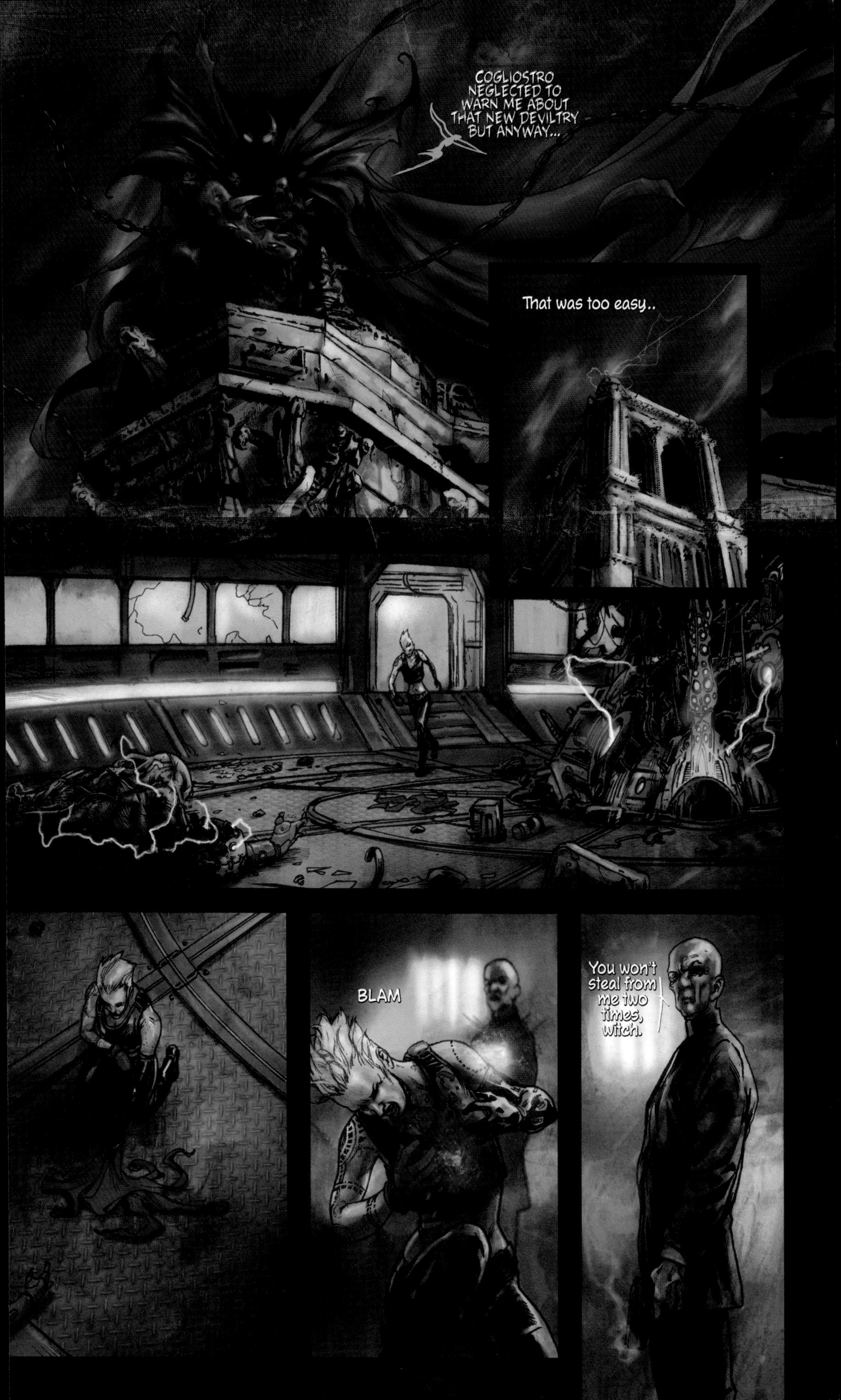
COGLIOSTRO NEGLECTED TO WARN ME ABOUT THAT NEW DEVILTRY BUT ANYWAY...
That was too easy..
BLAM
You won't steal from me two times, witch.

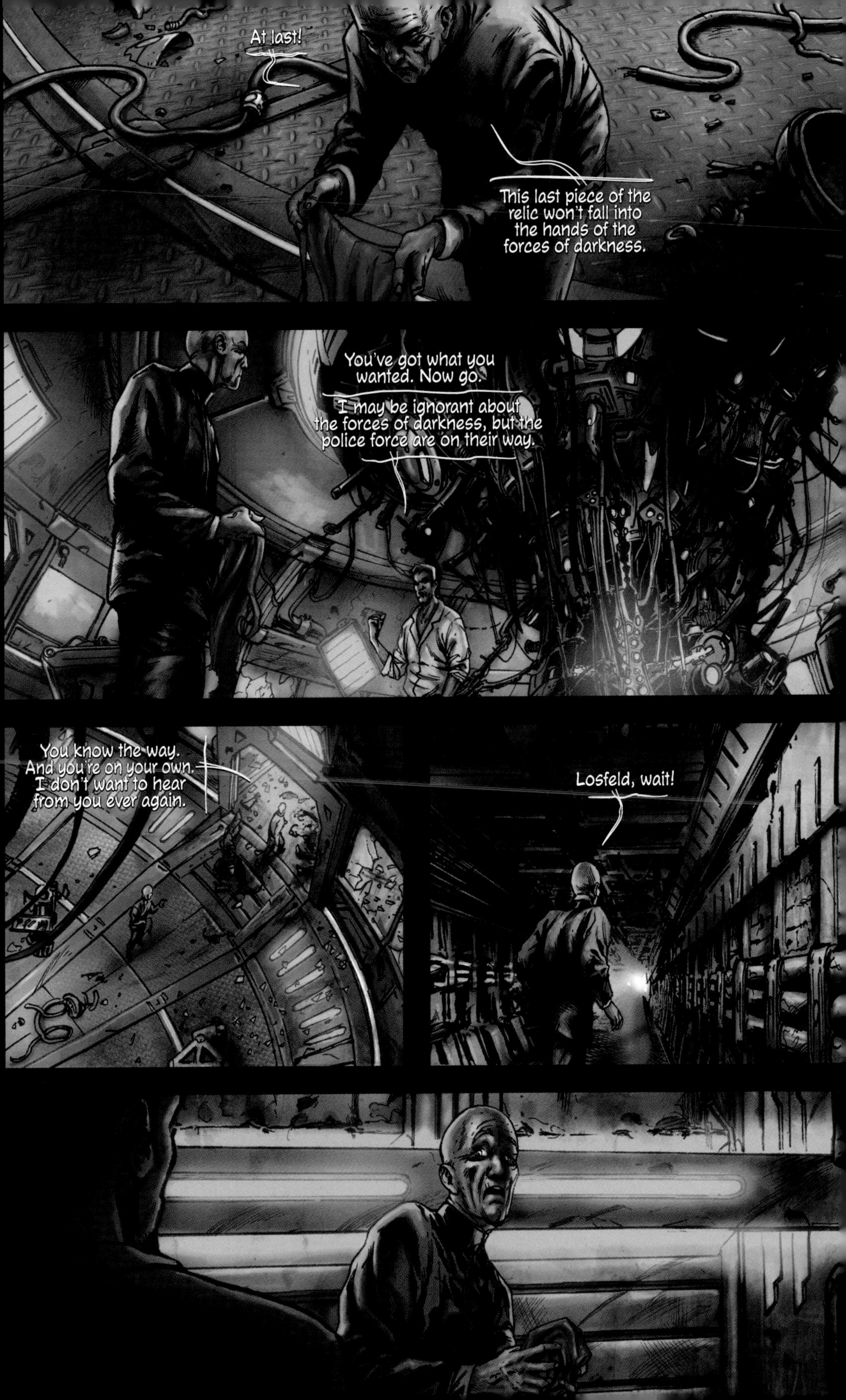
At last!
This last piece of the relic won't fall into the hands of the forces of darkness.
You've got what you wanted. Now go.
I may be ignorant about the forces of darkness, but the police force are on their way.
You know the way. And you're on your own. I don't want to hear from you ever again.
Losfeld, wait!

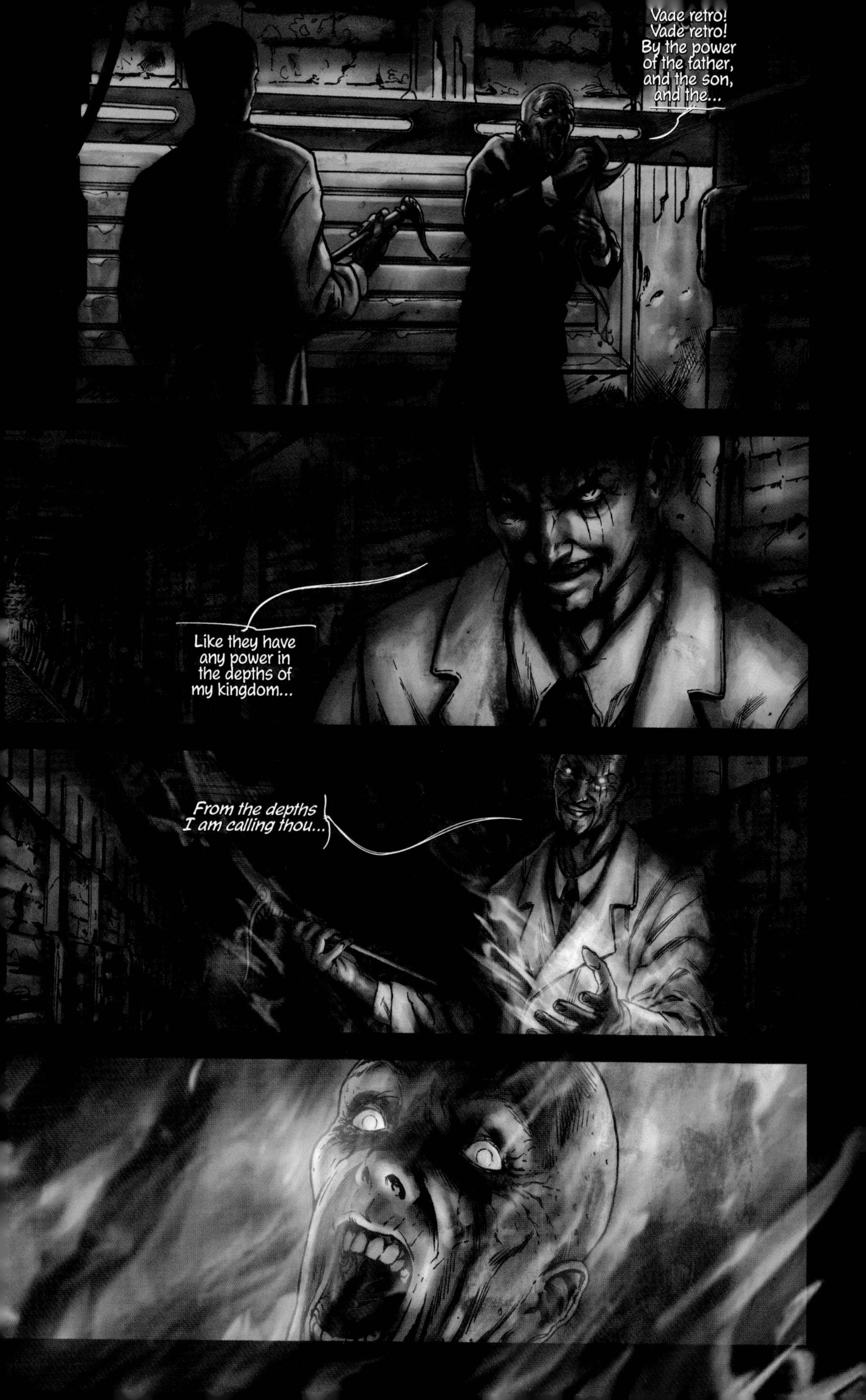
Vaae retro! Vade retro! By the power of the father, and the son, and the...
Like they have any power in the depths of my kingdom...
From the depths I am calling thou...

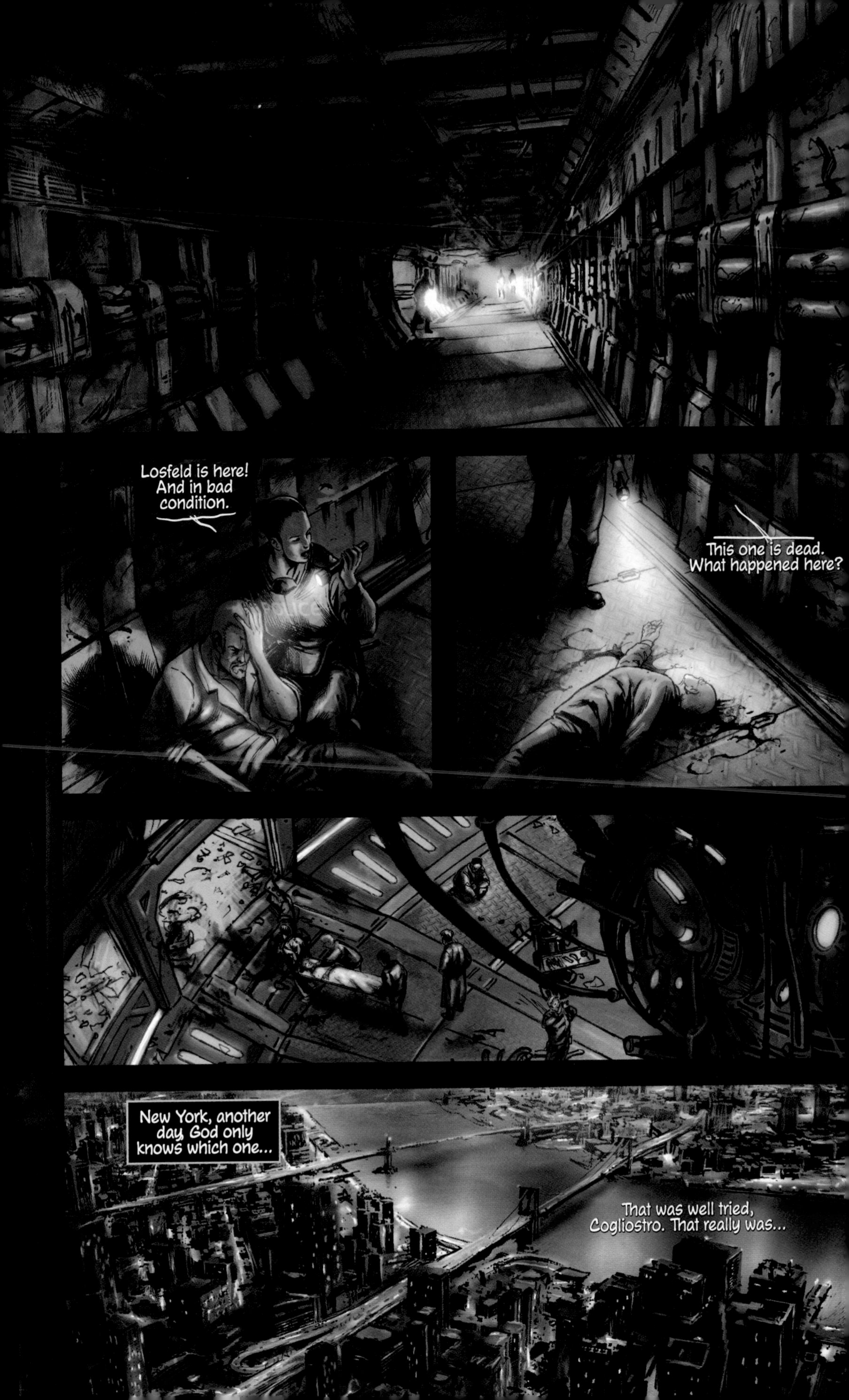
Losfeld is here! And in bad condition.
This one is dead. What happened here?
New York, another day. God only knows which one...
That was well tried, Cogliostro. That really was...

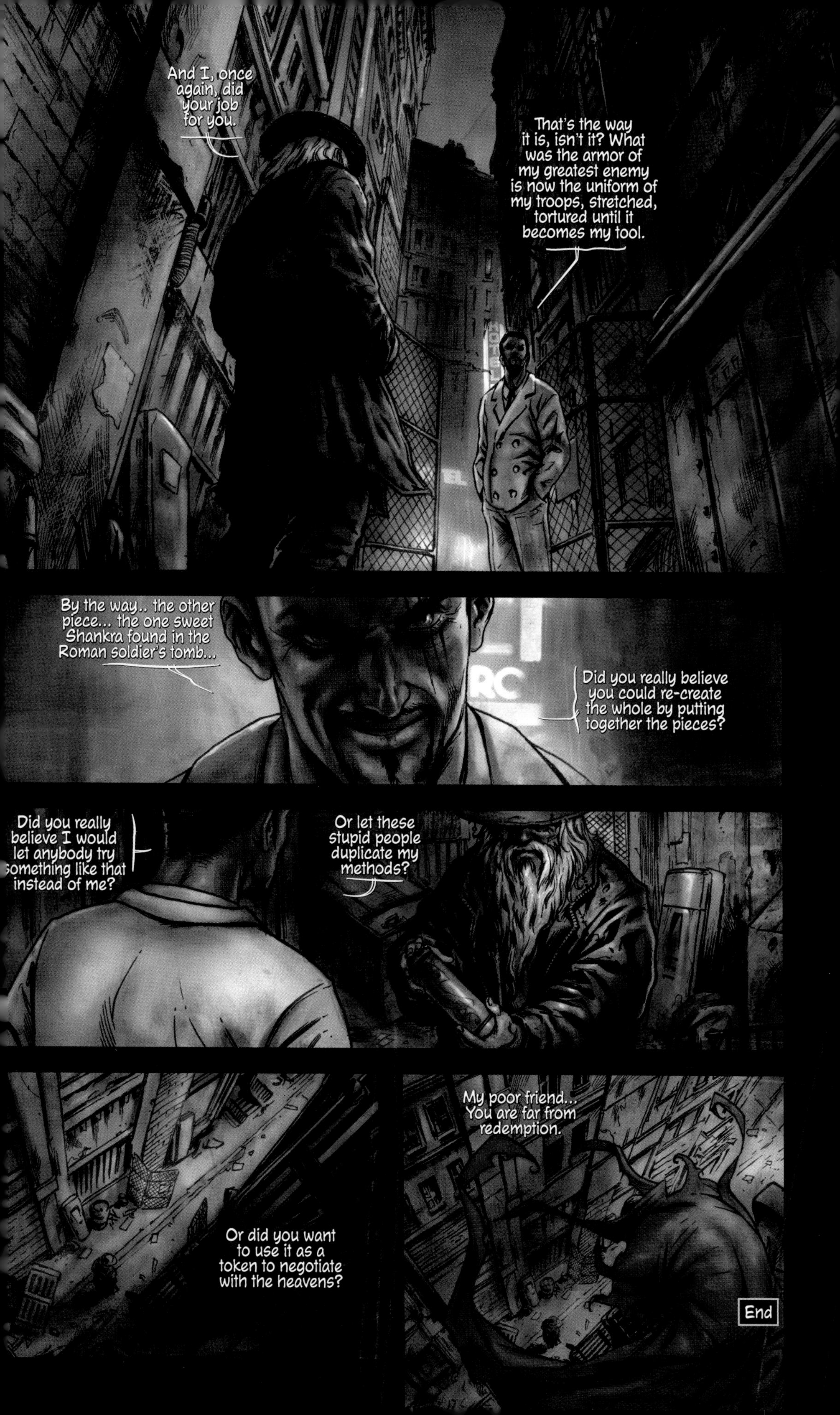

And I, once again, did your job for you.
That's the way it is, isn't it? What was the armor of my greatest enemy is now the uniform of my troops, stretched, tortured until it becomes my tool.
HOTEL
By the way.. the other piece... the one sweet Shankra found in the Roman soldier's tomb...
Did you really believe you could re-create the whole by putting together the pieces?
Did you really believe I would let anybody try something like that instead of me?
Or let these stupid people duplicate my methods?
Or did you want to use it as a token to negotiate with the heavens?
My poor friend... You are far from redemption.
End

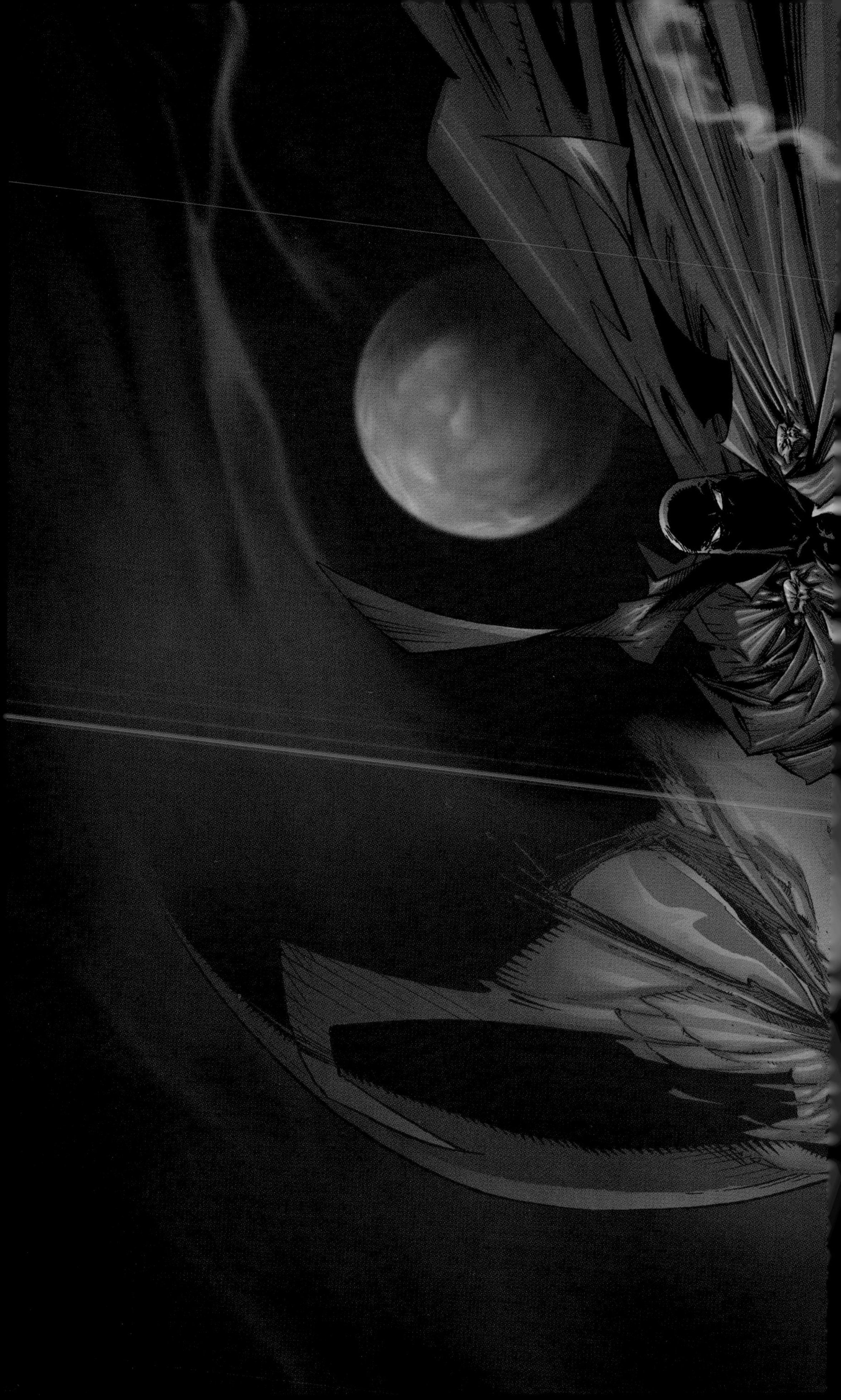

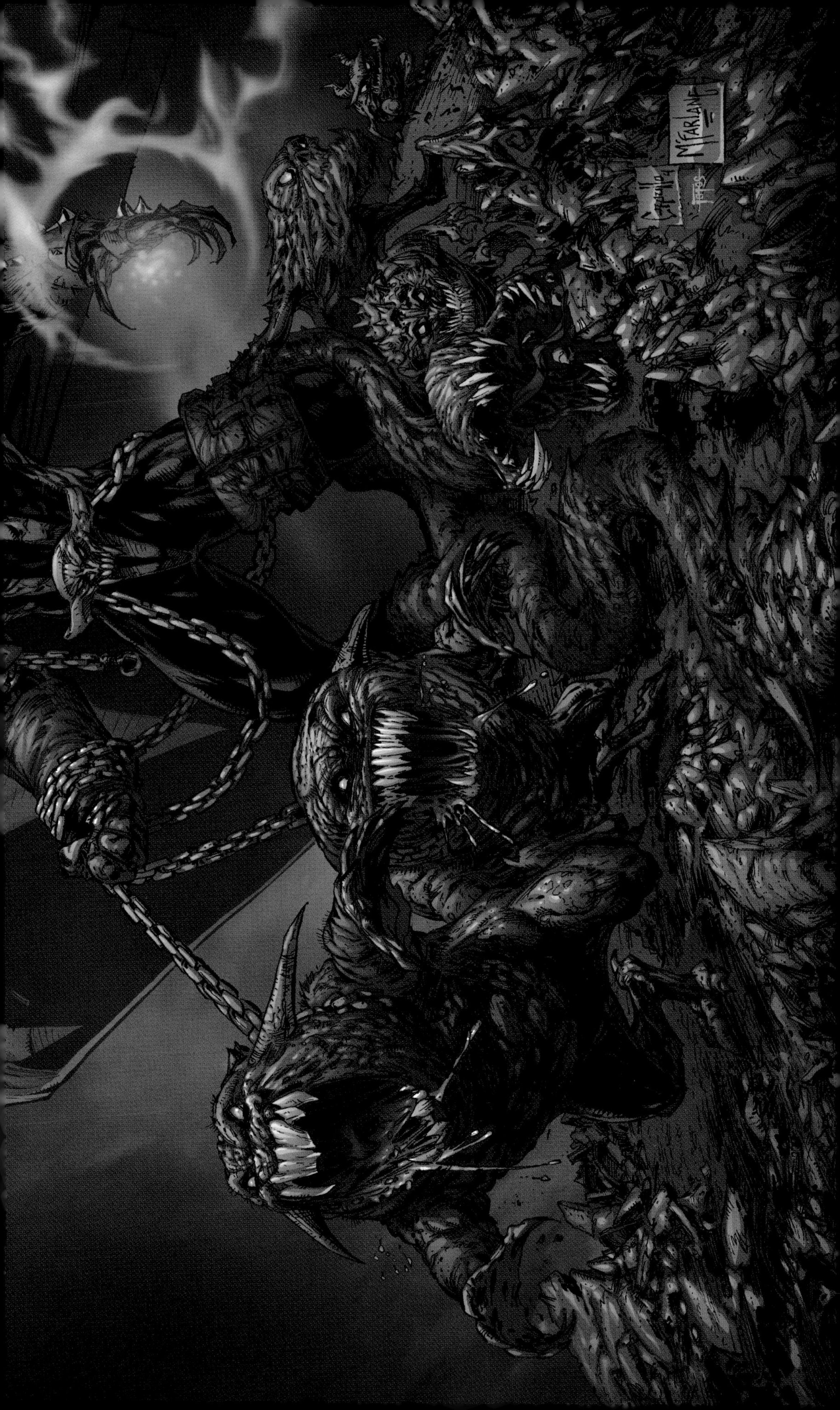

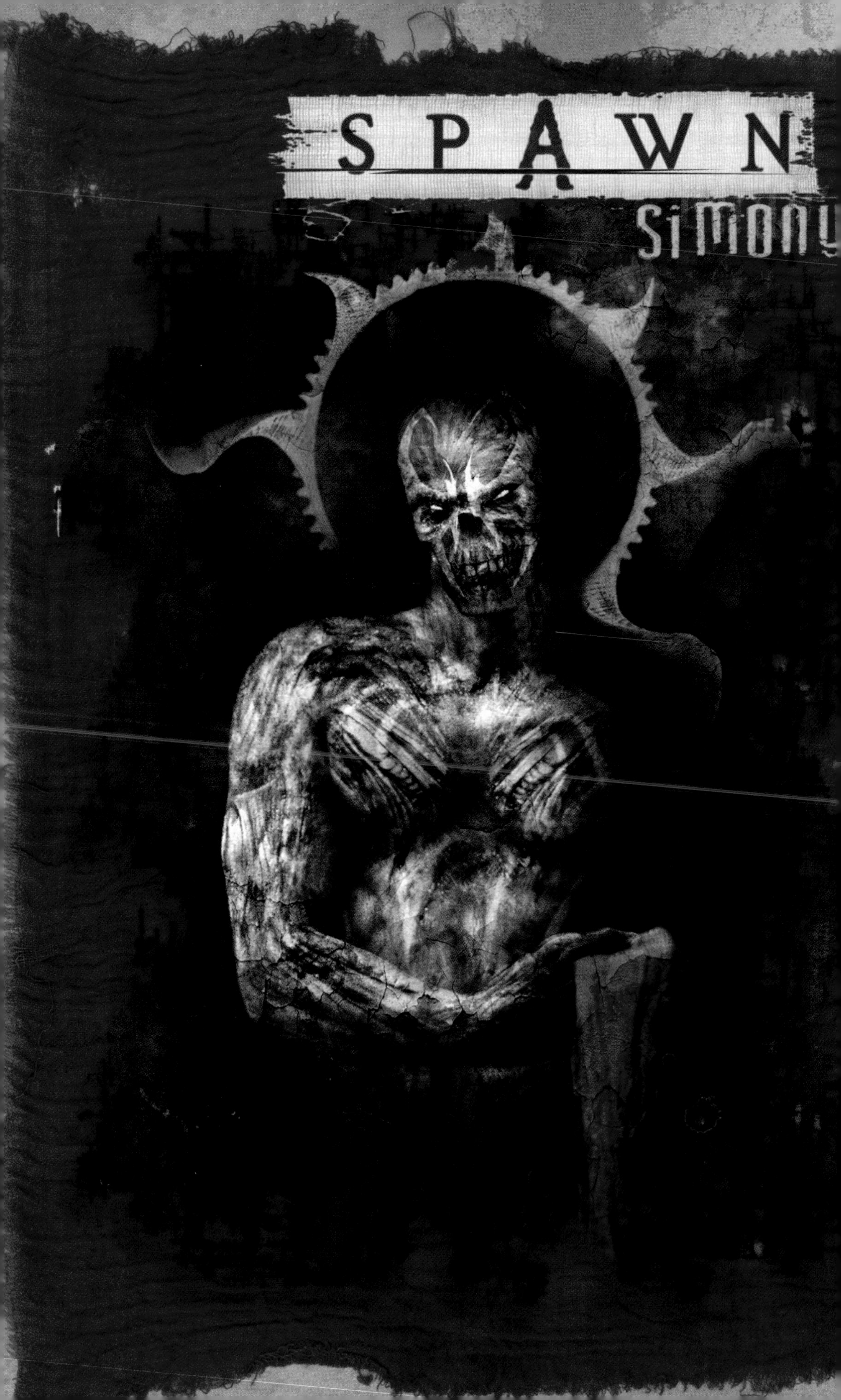
SPAWN
SIMONY

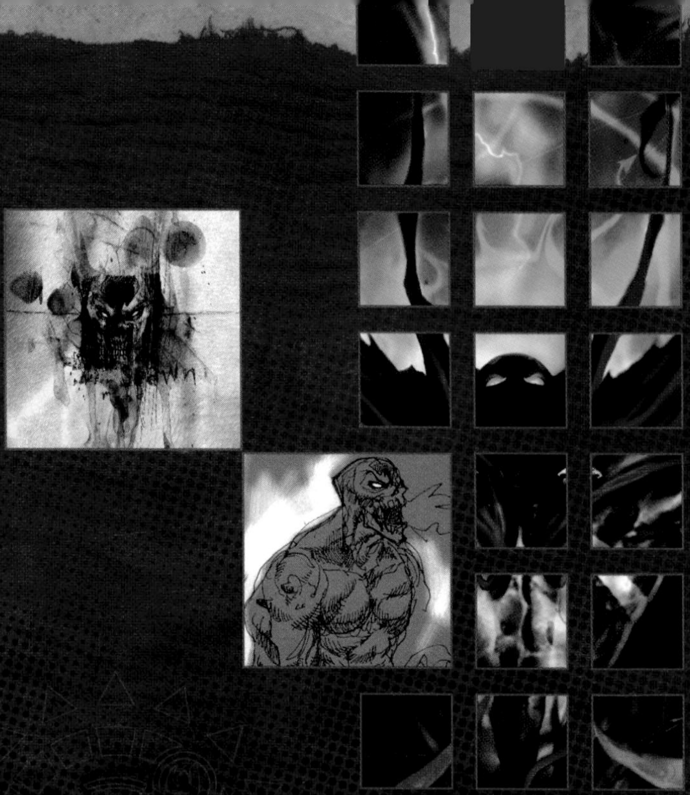

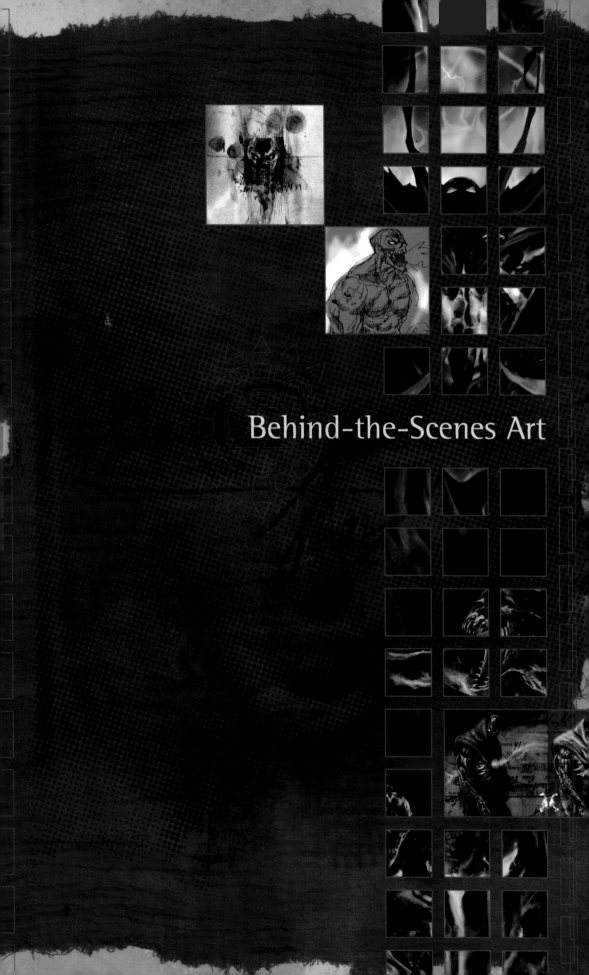

Behind-the-Scenes Art

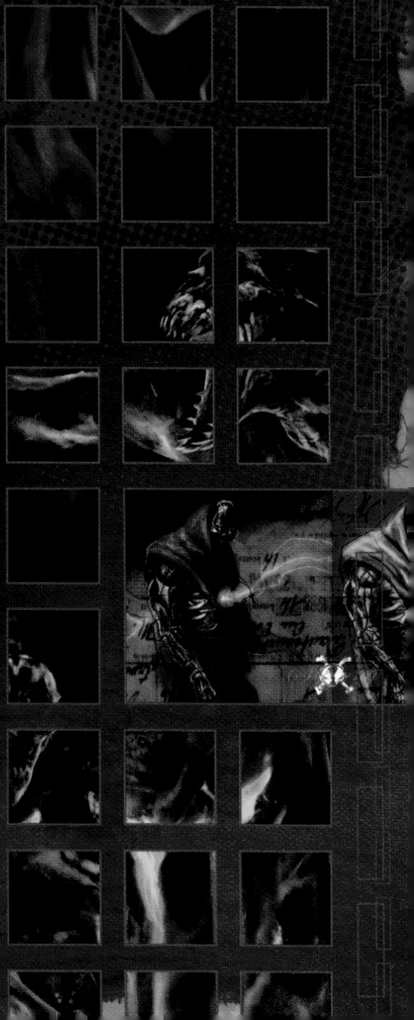

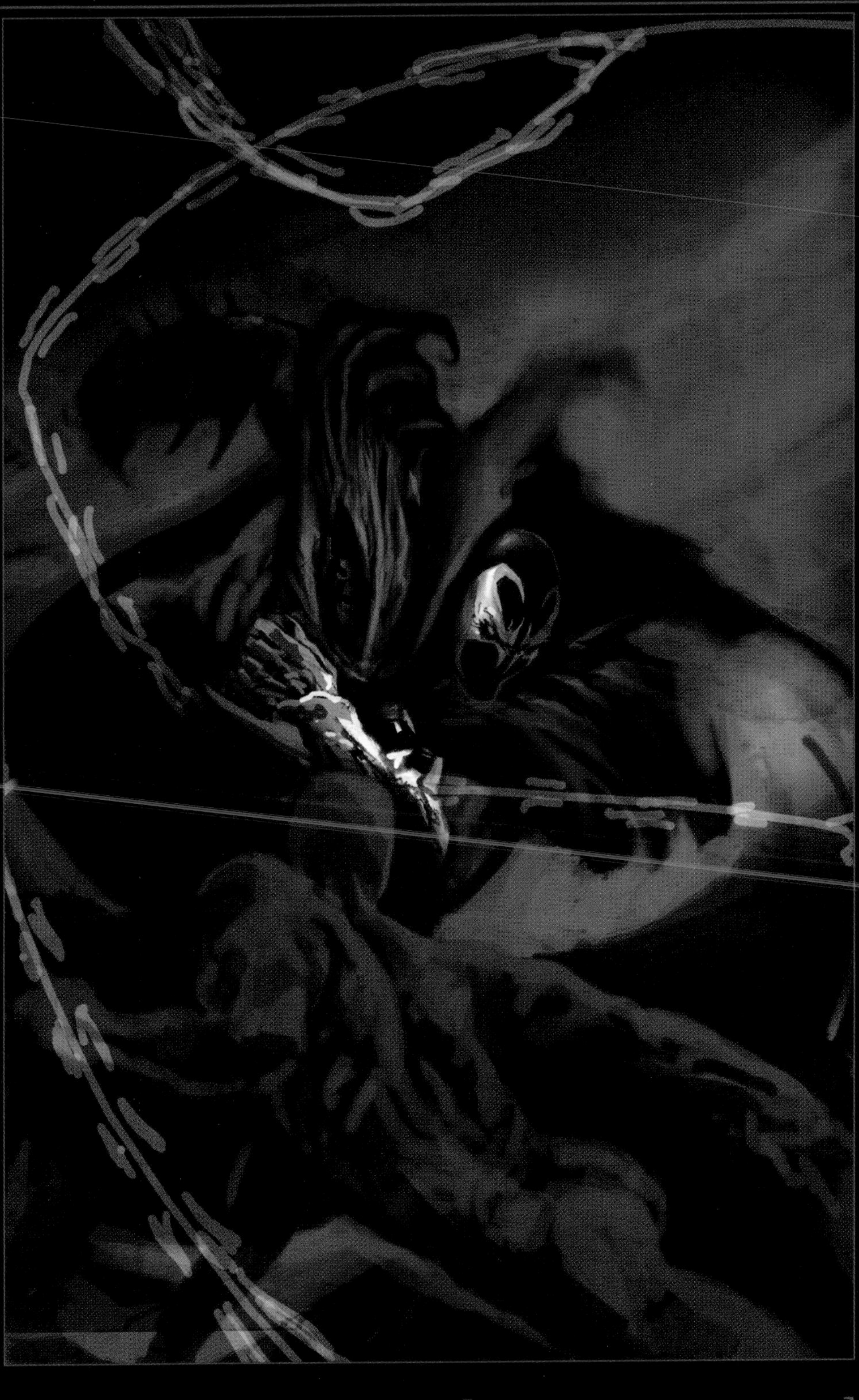

Rejected Cover Project for SPAWN: SIMONY

OW: A Hellspawn-ish piece of artwork by **ALEKSI BRICLOT** similar in style to Ben Templesmith

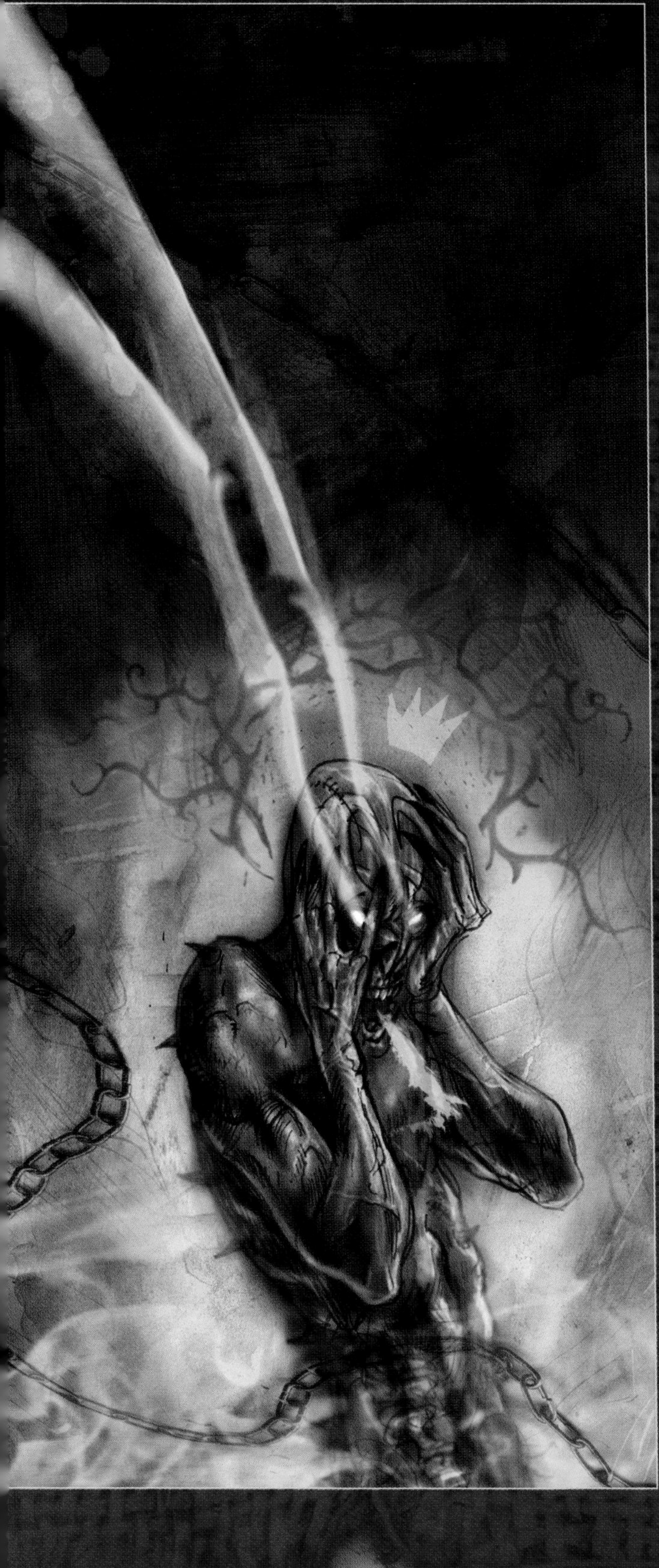

Aleksi tries to draw Spawn in a style similar to the core **SPAWN** comic by Angel Medina and Greg Capullo. It's very difficult to create your own version of an existing character without copying what was done by the previous artists.

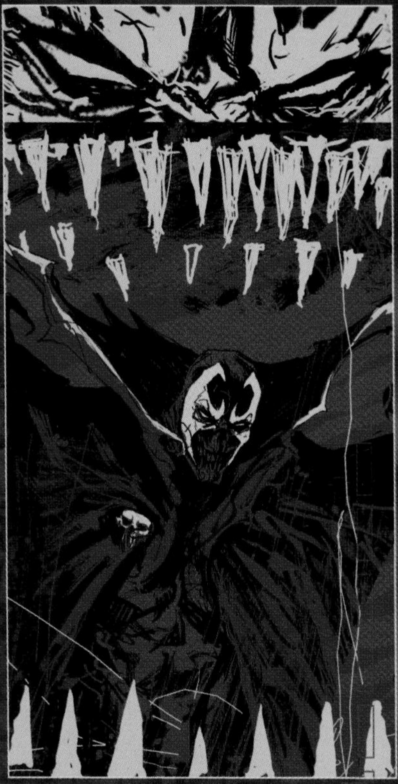

ABOVE: Aleksi demonstrates his ability to adapt, illustrating the same character in different styles.

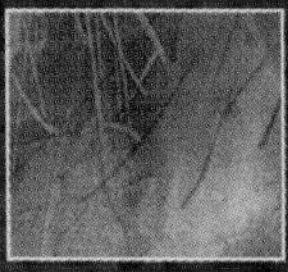

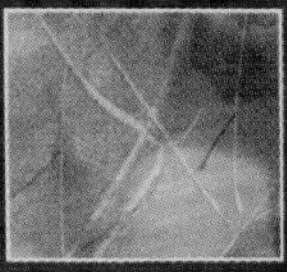

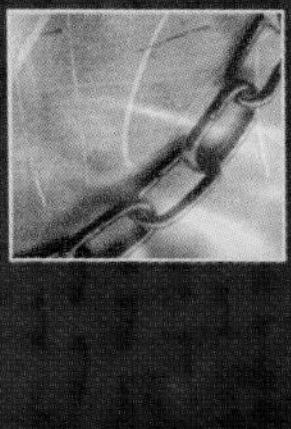

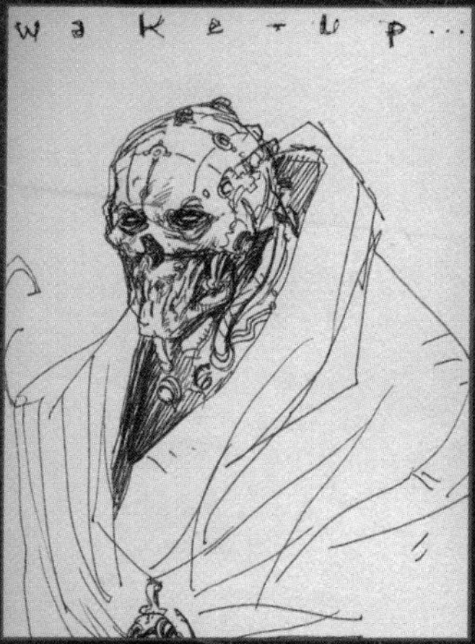
wake up...

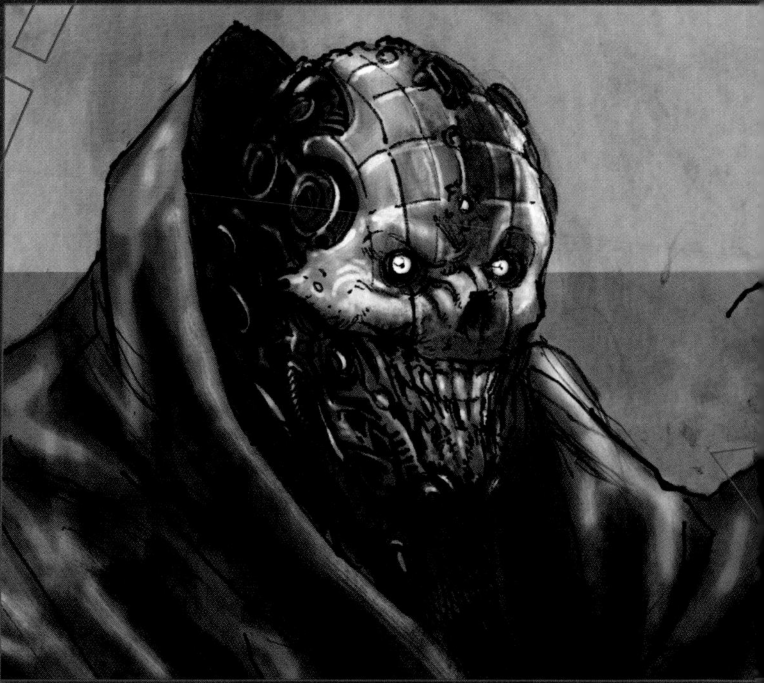

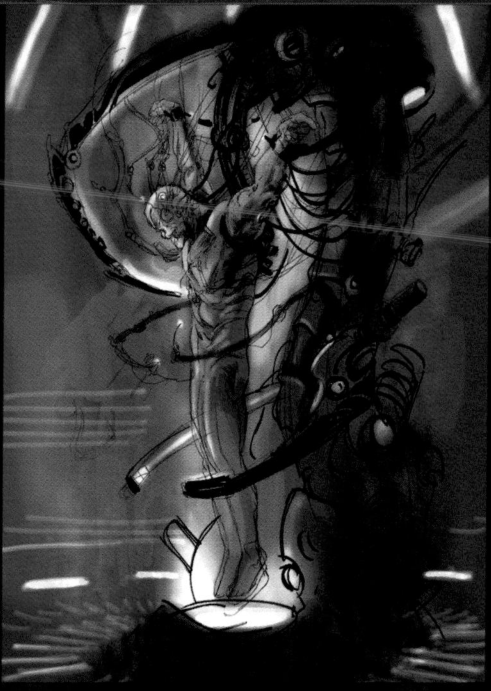

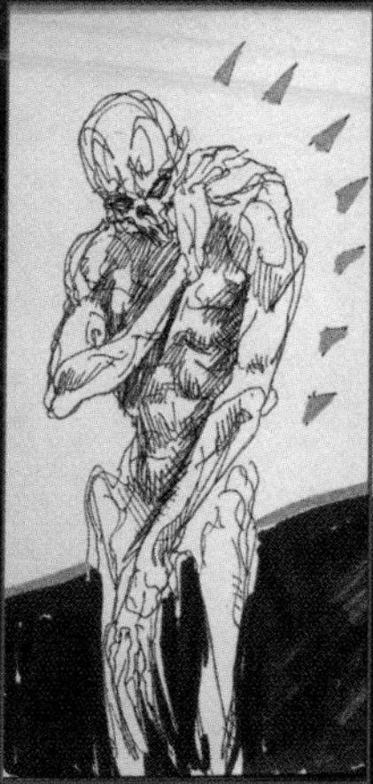

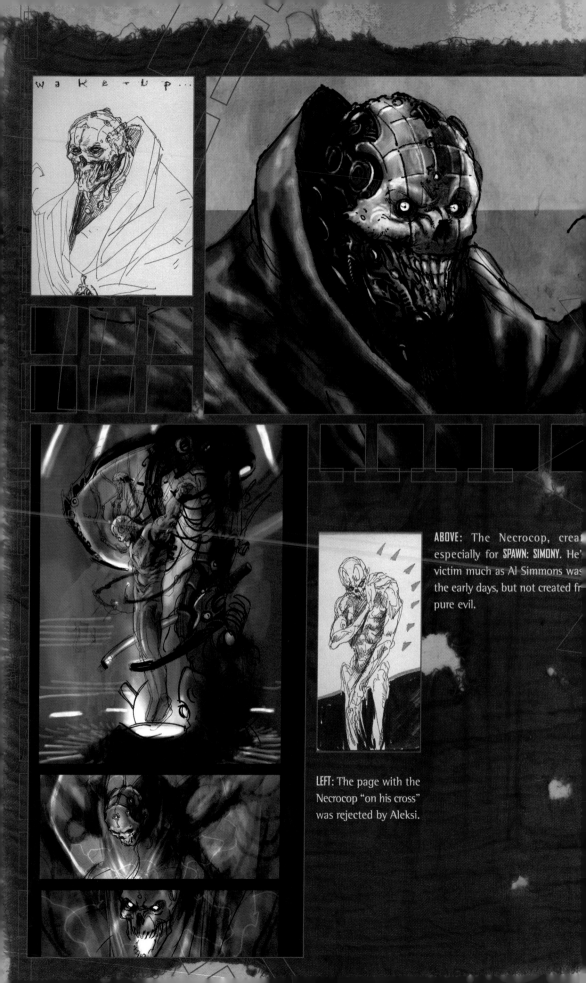

ABOVE: The Necrocop, crea
especially for **SPAWN: SIMONY**. He'
victim much as Al Simmons was
the early days, but not created fr
pure evil.

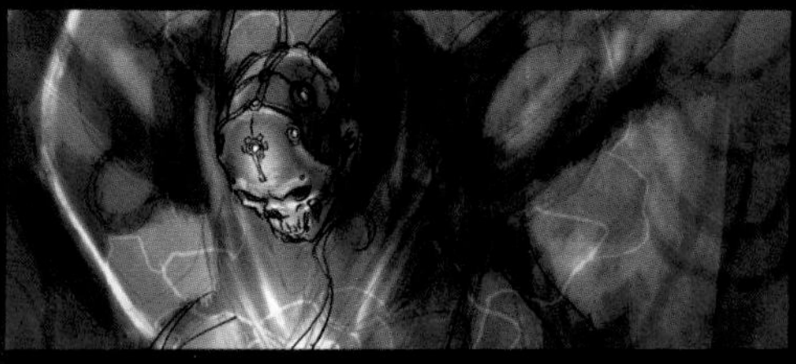

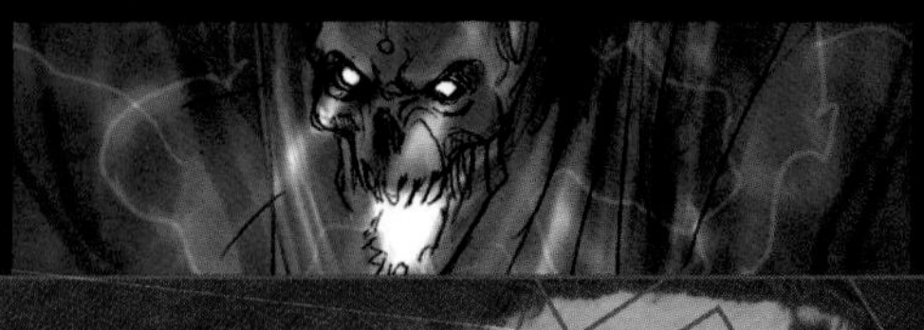

LEFT: The page with the Necrocop "on his cross" was rejected by Aleksi.

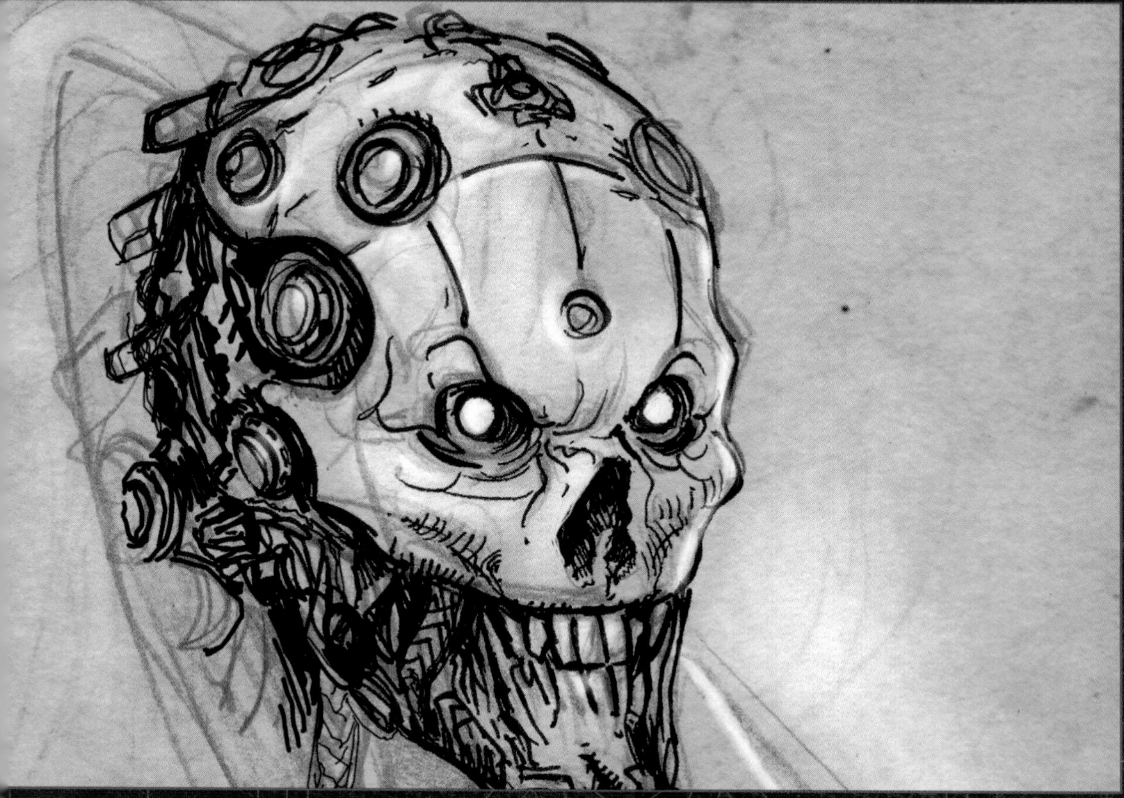

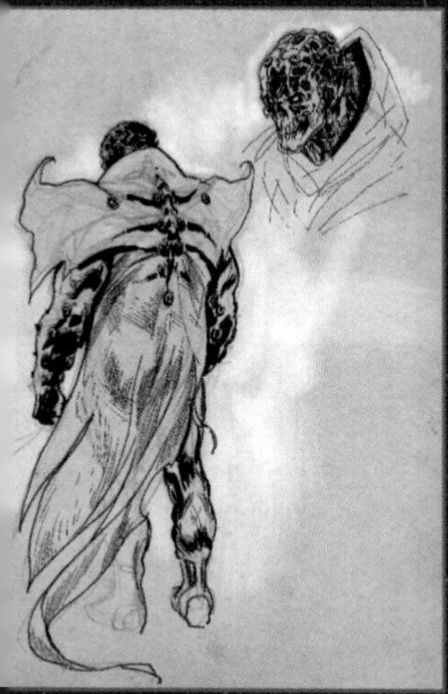

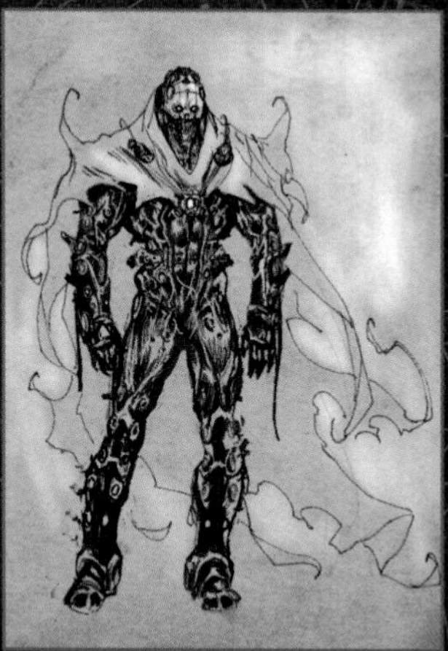

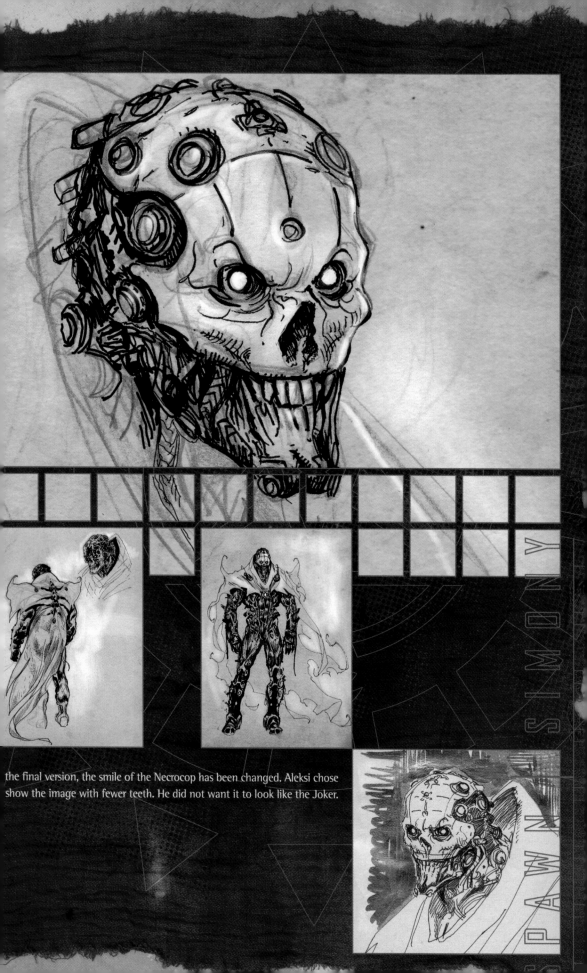

the final version, the smile of the Necrocop has been changed. Aleksi chose show the image with fewer teeth. He did not want it to look like the Joker.

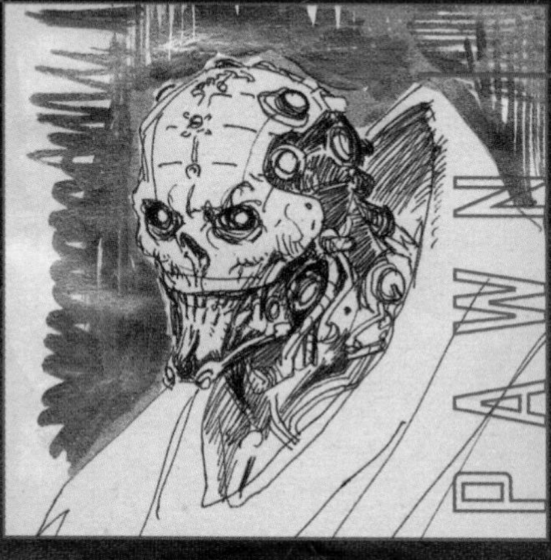

SPAWN SIMONY

Four pages of storyboards as they were designed by Aleksi before shipping for approval at TMP. As you will see, the final pages are very close to these versions. All these pages are computerized pages drawn and colored by Aleksi.

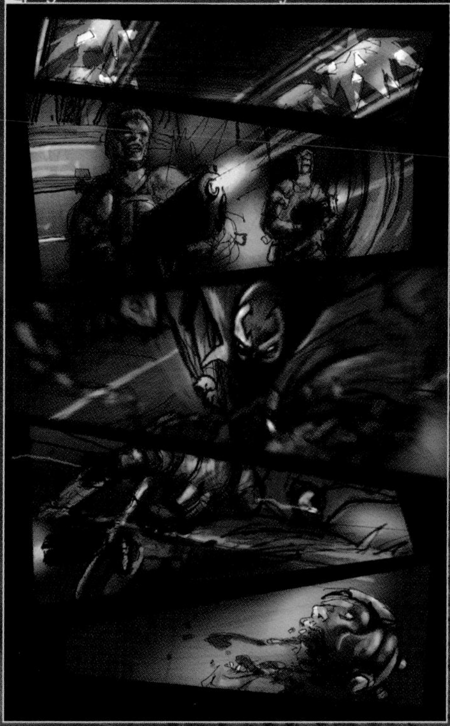

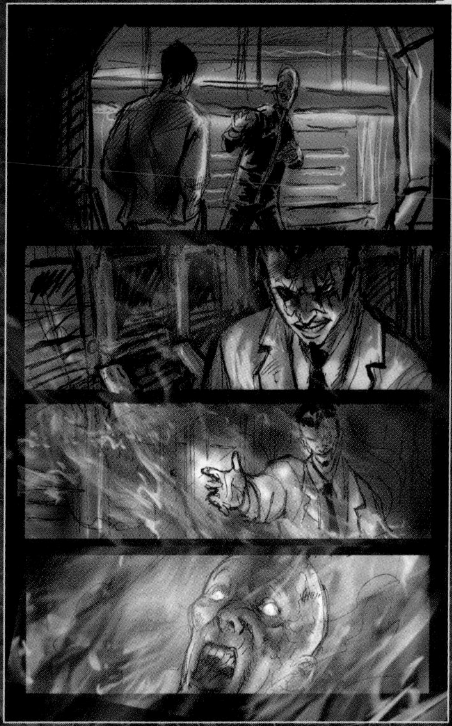

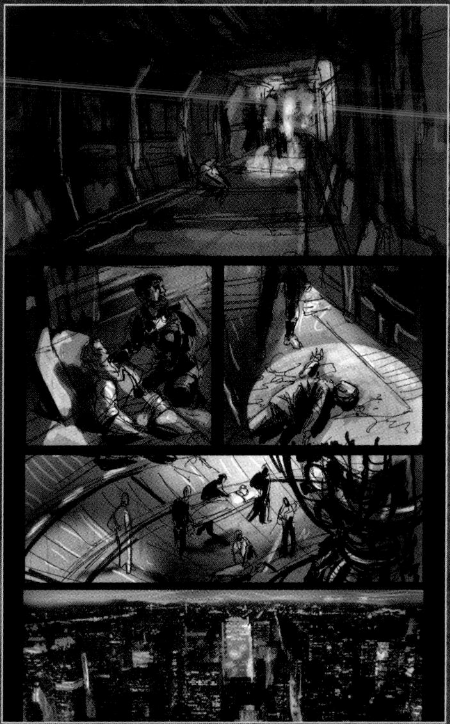

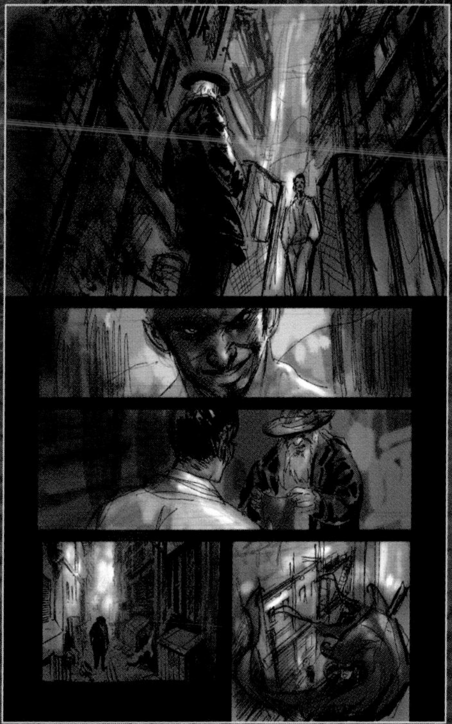

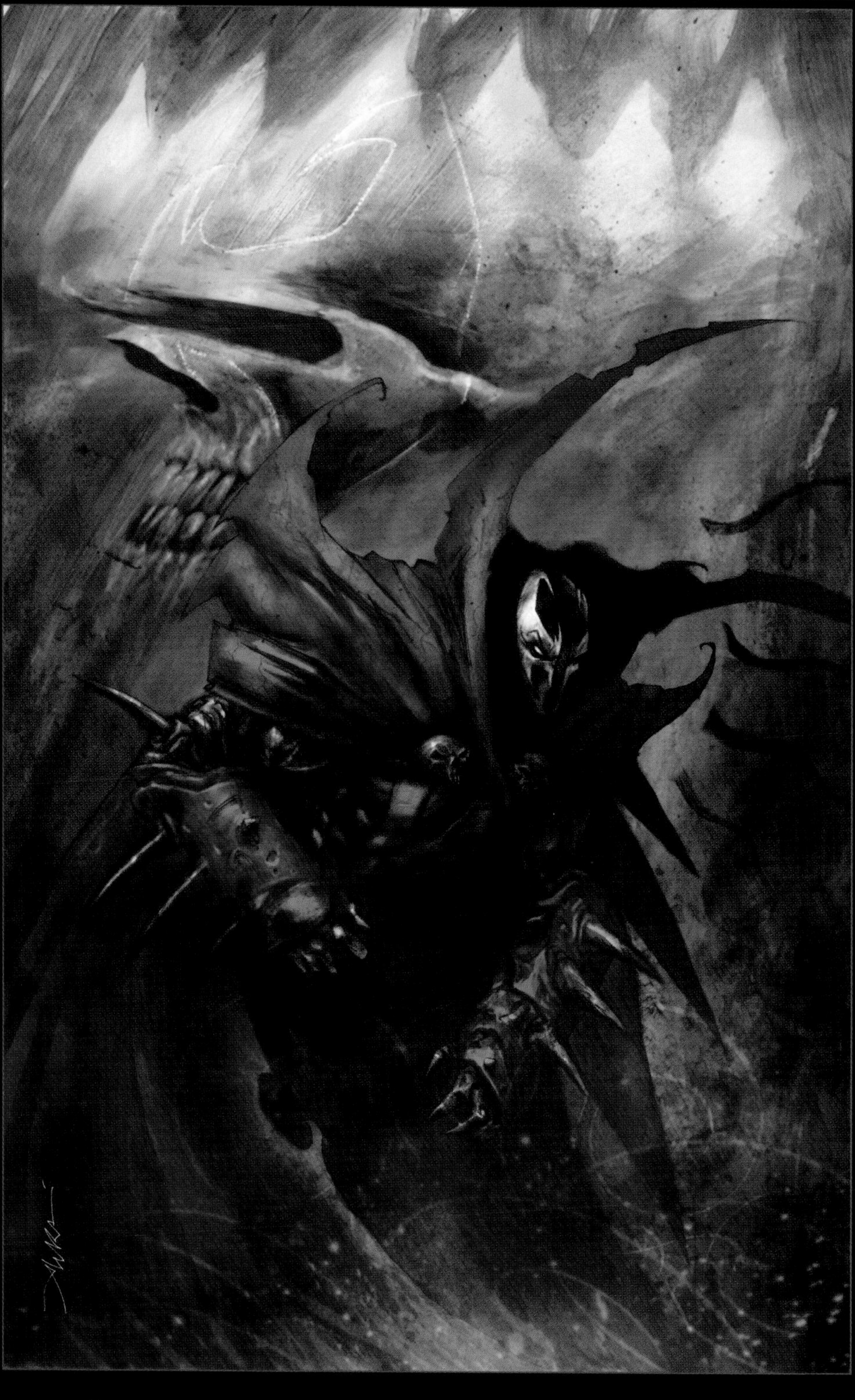

[This is one of the initial rough sketches done by **SPAWN: SIMONY** artist Aleksi Briclot soon after the French Spawn project was announced.]

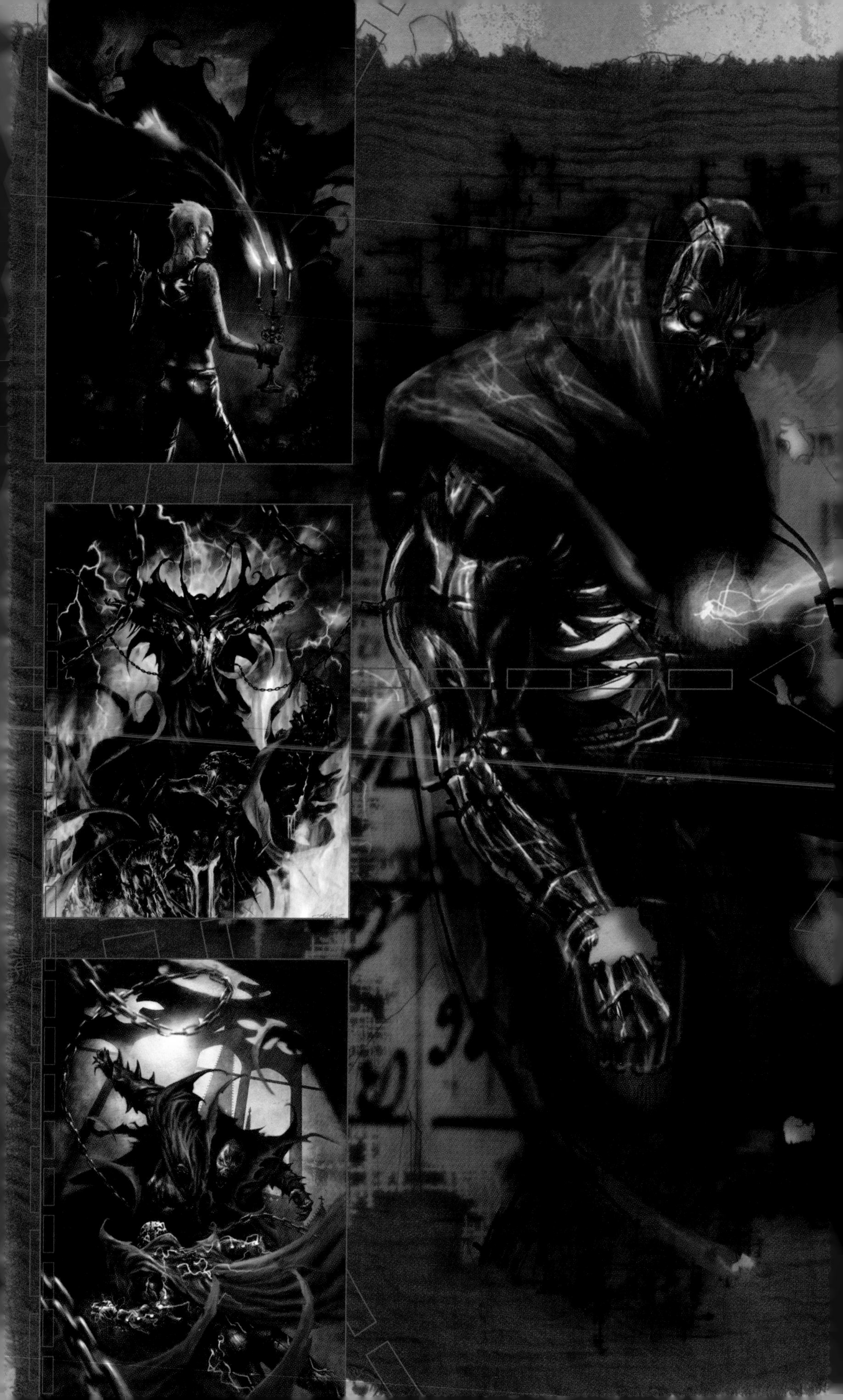

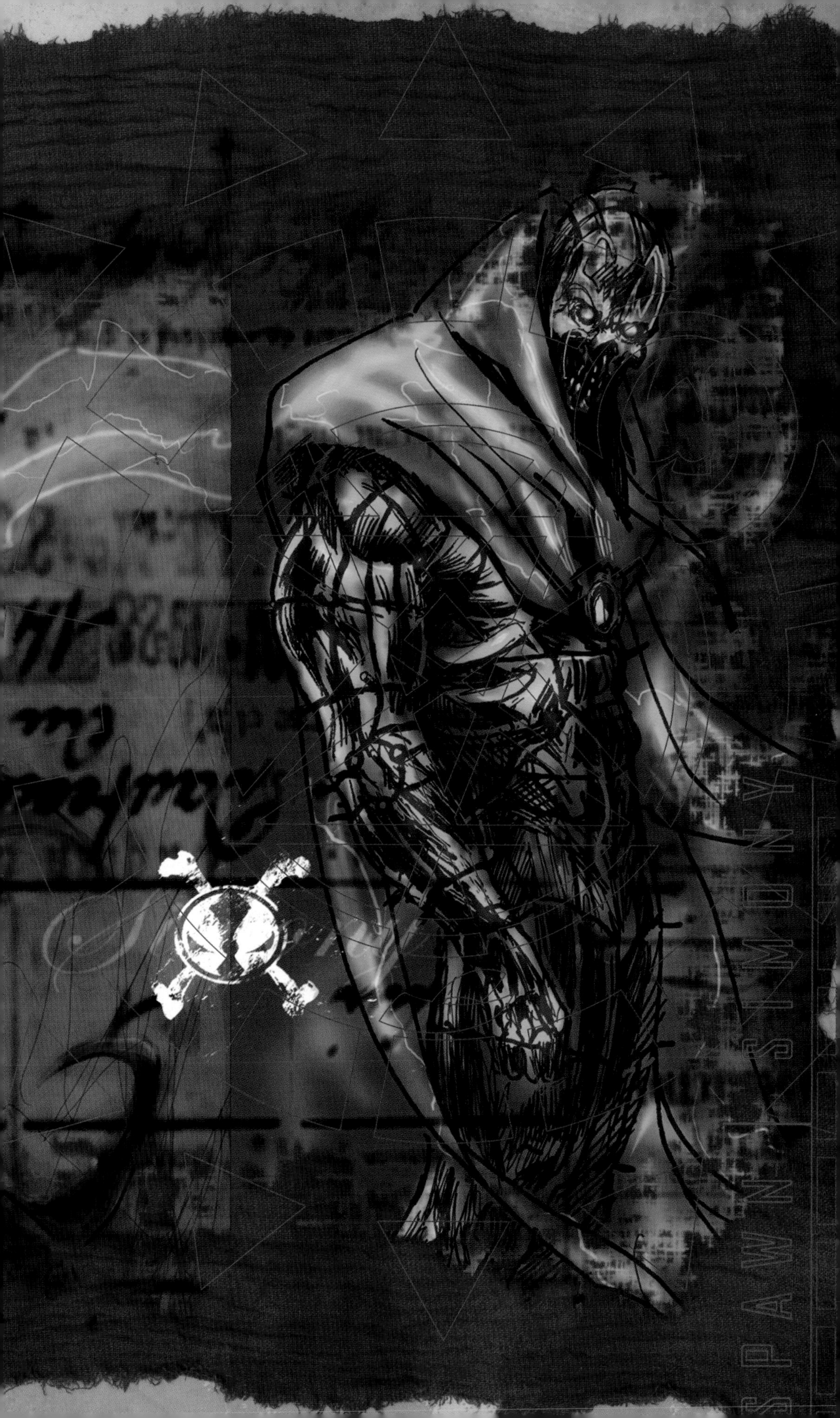
SPAWN SIMONY

SEMIC STUDIOS

ALEKSI BRICLOT

This 24-year-old Parisian artist usually works in the video game industry both as concept artist and art director. He has drawn hundreds of illustrations for books, RPG books, posters and magazines, and also appeared in the 10th issue of the fantastic art anthology. He won the 2003 conceptart.org Terminator 3 Art Contest. His first work in comics was the adaptation of the video game *Alone in the Dark*, published by Image Comics in the U.S. Aleksi has always felt comfortable with the Spawn universe's gothic, graphic mood. Since *Spawn: Simony*, he has worked on two different European hardcover projects to be released in 2004. He is currently developing a huge horror-action video game for Darkworks.

ALEX NIKOLAVITCH

This French/Serbian writer lives near Paris. Besides *Spawn: Simony*, his writing credits include *Central Zero*, a hardcover graphic novel published last year. Alex is very prolific with many short stories to his credit. He has also translated many comic books, including *Hellspawn*. Outside the comic book field, he has been a chemist, a radio speaker, a bookstore clerk and a newspaper journalist. He is currently working on several graphic novels, including a World War II story and the graphic biography of an urban shaman known as Hors Humain. He described *Spawn: Simony* as a unique opportunity to work on the American comic book format, a childhood dream.

THIERRY MORNET

Semic Editor-in-Chief was born in Paris, has lived in England and Germany, and became a comic book editor as sweet revenge against his parents who didn't want him to read comic books when he was a kid. He's developed a real passion for US comics as well as manga or the so-called French Bande Dessinée, hence the "French Touch Project" developed for a couple of years in which *Spawn: Simony* is one of the main achievements to date. He lives near Paris with his wife and two kids and is currently looking for a larger flat to store all his comics.

JEAN-FRANÇOIS PORCHEROT

Semic Editor, discovered comics in high school and never dreamt it could become a job. He worked first with motorcycle racers then joined an R&D computer company developing palmtops including handwriting recognition. This job gave him the opportunity to attend the Comdex Show in Las Vegas, where he found *Spawn #1*. His previous credits in the comic book field include the release of the first *Manara* statue and a 1997 Diamond award for a *Hellboy* resin statue. At Comdex he met Thierry Mornet who recruited him to handle all TMP titles at Semic. Never say never.

TODD McFARLANE PRODUCTIONS

TODD McFARLANE

Born in Canada in 1961, McFarlane's road trip to creative autonomy began when he accepted an assignment penciling for Marvel/Epic Comics in March 1984. From there, he worked his way to the top of the talent roster before leaving Marvel to help found Image Comics with six other artists.

It was then that Todd introduced his own character, Spawn. The book's debut in 1992 sold an amazing 1.7 million copies, an unprecedented feat in independent comics. From there came a whirlwind of growth and expansion: more comics, action figures, spawn.com, film and animation.

In 1994, Todd founded McFarlane Toys, because he wanted to maintain maximum creative control over his Spawn character. Over the years, the company has become one of the largest, most renowned toy manufacturers in the world. In addition to Spawn, McFarlane Toys has produced figures from dozens of outside properties, including all four major North American sports, Clive Barker, *KISS, Shrek, X-Files, Austin Powers, The Beatles, Army of Darkness, Jaws, Rob Zombie, Alien, Predator, Terminator 3, The Matrix* and many others.

Todd is still heavily involved in the *Spawn* comic book, which today is on issue #135.

GREG CAPULLO

Self taught, Greg Capullo is perhaps best known as the artist for the Todd McFarlane Productions flagship comic book *Spawn*. Originally slated for a three-issue story arc, Greg's run on *Spawn* lasted from issue 16 to issue 100. Along the way, Greg has worked on various other projects for Marvel, Image, Dark Horse and Chaos! In 1997, Greg released his own book, *The Creech*, which was well-received by fans. In July 2001, the next installment of *The Creech: Out For Blood* was published by Todd McFarlane Productions. Currently, Greg pencils covers for *Spawn, Case Files: Sam and Twitch* and other special projects. His Web site is www.thecreech.com.

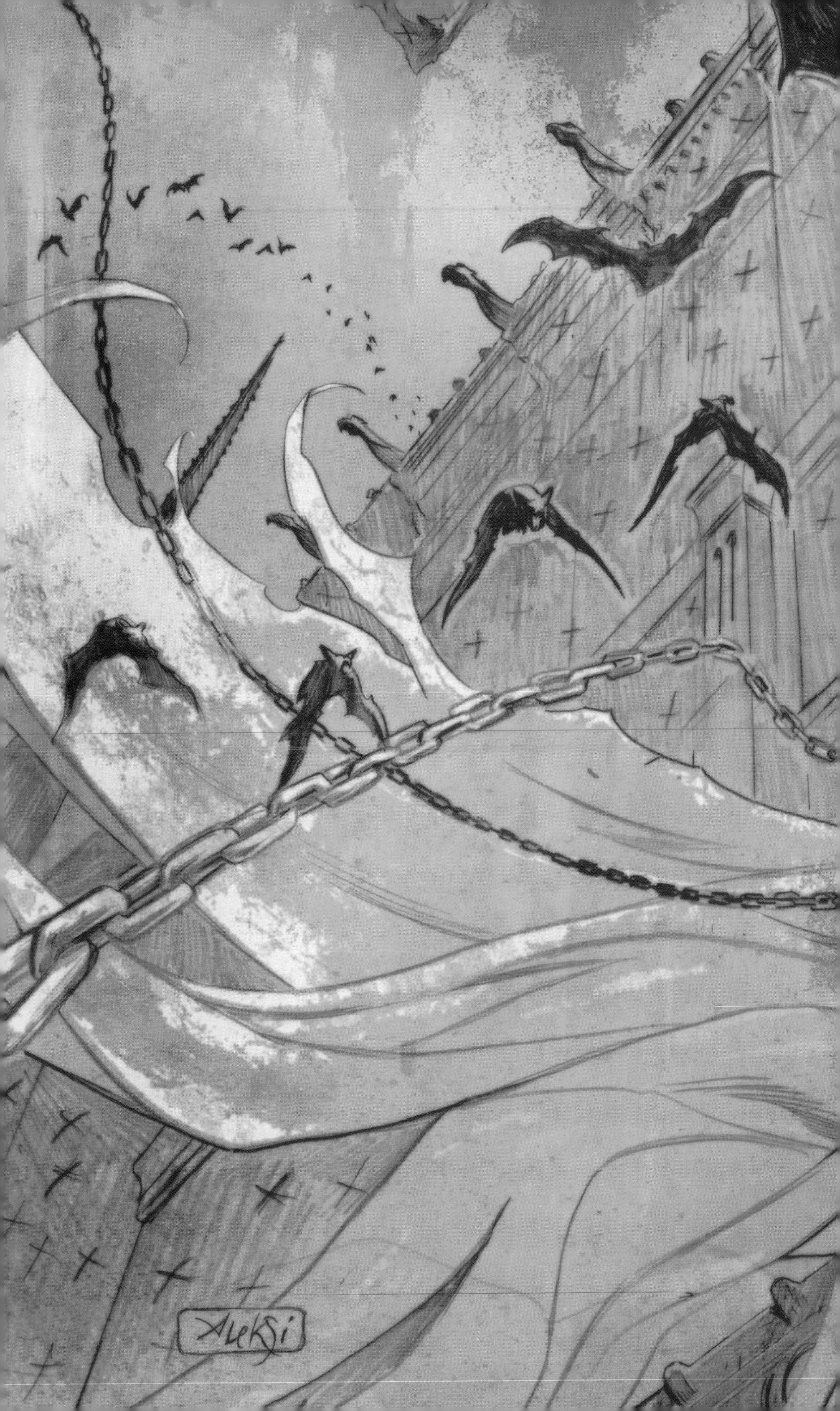
Aleksi